Bardot

Bardot

Sean French

PAVILION

A Molly, mon bébé

First published in Great Britain in 1994 by
PAVILION BOOKS LIMITED
26 Upper Ground, London SE1 9PD

Designed by
The Bridgewater Book Company/Chris Dymond

Picture research by Juliet Brightmore

A CIP catalogue record for this book
is available from the British Library.

ISBN 1 85793 3486 (hbk)
ISBN 1 85793 5853 (pbk)

Printed and bound in Great Britain by
Butler & Tanner Ltd., Frome and London

2 4 6 8 10 9 7 5 3 1

This book may be ordered by post
direct from the publisher. Please contact
the Marketing Department.
But try your bookshop first.

Contents

*I*ntroduction

PAGE 6

*B*ébé

PAGE 22

*A*nd Vadim Created Bardot

PAGE 38

*A*fter the Creation

PAGE 54

*P*rivate Lives

PAGE 80

*J*e me donne à qui me plaît

PAGE 114

*I*f Don Juan Were a Woman

PAGE 140

*A*nimals

PAGE 160

*F*ilmography

PAGE 184

*I*ndex

PAGE 188

*A*cknowledgements

PAGE 192

Introduction

*I*t was Roger Vadim who discovered Brigitte Bardot. When she was fifteen, he was sent to see her after her picture had appeared on the cover of *Elle*. In a confused sequence he fell in love with her, married her, got her into films and, at the very moment he was losing her, made her the most famous screen actress in the world. If anybody can see Bardot clearly and directly, it ought to be Vadim. Yet when he came to write a ruefully adoring, baffled memoir of her, he began it in a curious way. His vivid opening image is not of first meeting her, marrying her or directing her, but of a publicity stunt that he staged at the Cannes Film Festival in 1953, when she had appeared in just one film, a minor rural comedy called *Le Trou Normand (Crazy for Love; Ti Ta To)*. She announced her arrival at the festival by visiting the United States aircraft carrier, *Enterprise*, then at anchor in the Bay of Cannes. Vadim describes this unknown young actress as she must have appeared to the sailors who were seeing her for the first time:

First they saw her long tresses floating on the surface of the water; then her face, streaming with drops of water, glistening in the sun like so many diamonds. Her innocent, sensual mouth and perfect

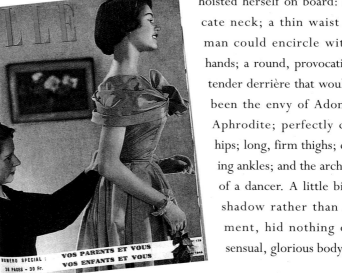

oval eyes, her delicate nose, her cheeks as round as a child's, were made for pleasure and laughter. Two hands with aristocratic wrists gripped the edge of the Chris-Craft and the apparition hoisted herself on board: a delicate neck; a thin waist that a man could encircle with two hands; a round, provocative and tender derrière that would have been the envy of Adonis and Aphrodite; perfectly curved hips; long, firm thighs; charming ankles; and the arched feet of a dancer. A little bikini, a shadow rather than a garment, hid nothing of this sensual, glorious body.

The blurb on the dust jacket of another of Vadim's memoirs asserts that his 'liaisons with a series of beautiful women have provoked envy and admiration' and it is evident that this envy and admiration, the imagination of the onlooker, was as important to Vadim himself as it was to the gawping public, the paparazzi and the cinema-goers in the world outside. The public felt they were only seeing Bardot on screen whereas Roger Vadim possessed the real thing, the woman herself. It was part of Vadim's narrow genius to perceive that the opposite was true. The 'real' Bardot was the erotic image and

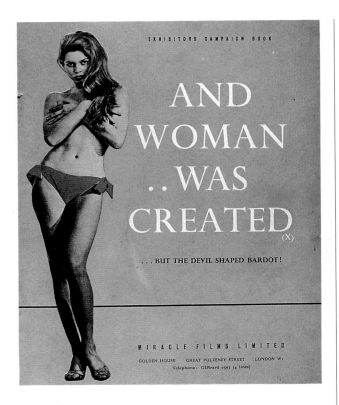

ABOVE

Bardot glowers at her English public on a poster for the film that made her world famous

Vadim – Bardot's lover and mentor – had to fantasize about being one of us, the people who saw her on screen or from a distance, in order properly to possess her, or the idea of her. What was exciting was not so much the intrinsic details of his wife's body in themselves but the idea of their being looked at by others. Michael Frayn has written that 'No woman is so naked as one you can see to be naked underneath her clothes' and Brigitte Bardot

appeared most erotic to Roger Vadim when she was physically unavailable to him – in public, being directed, on a poster, and, in the end, leaving him.

When Simone de Beauvoir came to write her famous essay, 'Brigitte Bardot and the Lolita Syndrome', arguably the most brilliant analysis ever written of a film star, she also began by recounting her experience of watching people watching Bardot. She was sitting in a studio audience where Bardot was performing on the guitar for a television programme. The women in the audience were disdainful of her abilities and unimpressed even by her looks: 'She's not even pretty. She has the face of a housemaid.' The men were attracted to her, but they too made a show of giggling contemptously: 'Only two or three of us, among thirty or so spectators, thought her charming. Then she did an excellent classical dance number. "She *can* dance," the others admitted grudgingly. Once again I could observe that Brigitte Bardot was disliked in her own country.'

Before Bardot there were many actresses who had become eroticized objects. Mae West's lips were copied in the famous design of a sofa by Salvador Dali, and her name applied to the U.S. Navy life-jacket in acknowledgement of her figure. Rita Hayworth and Veronica Lake's hair cascaded across their faces. Jane Russell, more overtly, was notorious for her bust, and it was claimed that her producer, Howard Hughes, had designed a specially cantilevered bra to support it. Roland Barthes wrote a celebrated essay on Greta Garbo's face, arguing that the actress 'still belongs to that moment when capturing the human face still plunged audiences into the deepest ecstasy'. In Marlene Dietrich's American films with Josef von Sternberg, sex was transformed from a biological urge into glorious artifice, not expressed and experienced by the body but portrayed in shadows, lighting and costume. Marilyn Monroe, with her hourglass shape, her bleached hair and breathless voice, was a cartoon of a sex symbol.

But there was no irony about Brigitte Bardot. She was the first actress whose attraction, whose fetishized sexuality, resided in her entire naked body: the long blond hair, the beautiful face with a mouth that only stopped pouting when it had to utter some (usually redundant) dialogue, and then the line down the back, across the curve of the buttocks and the long legs. *And God Created Woman (Et Dieu créa la femme)* startled film audiences from its very first scene (at least those who were able to see that scene in something like its original form). Without any gradual, teasing build-up, Bardot is

BELOW ————————————————

Brigitte Bardot presented a version of overt sexuality apparently lacking artifice or disguise — and often clothes

seen lying full-length and naked beneath the Mediterranean sun. This was in 1956, when the English-speaking cinema was still strictly censored and nudity for anybody except members of primitive tribes was ten years away. Somehow Brigitte Bardot had skipped a decade. With her long blond hair and her tanned, supple, unclothed body, she had invented the sixties six years before 1963 – the year in which, according to Philip Larkin, sexual intercourse was invented.

Bardot was as simple and uncontentious as sex itself – which means that she was not simple or uncontentious at all. Audiences could generally find some measure of agreement about film stars. When Kenneth Tynan wrote that 'what one sees in other women when drunk, one sees in Garbo sober', female movie-goers could see what he meant because he was talking about sex made deliriously abstract. Men as well as women adored Cary Grant, con-

fused perhaps about whether they were attracted to him or merely wanted to *be* him. There were occasional ripples of disagreement. The film critic, Alan Brien, once tetchily complained that he was tired of being told by gay male film critics that Lana Turner was not attractive.

Bardot divided, and continues to divide, audiences. In the final moments of one of her more trivial films, the 1957 comedy, *Une Parisienne (Parisienne)*, she turns and winks directly at the camera with sly complicity. Not everybody winks back. 'All the highbrows are on her side,' Marguerite Duras, herself a highbrow, insisted. To find some American equivalent for the attention paid to Bardot in the years after *And God Created Woman*, one would have to imagine essays on the young Raquel Welch

LEFT

The young Bardot, when cigarettes and sunshine were still good for you

by Hannah Arendt and Marianne Moore. Duras added: 'As for the public at large, they are split between the men who are all in love with her and the women who, sometimes, accept her.'

During the preparation of this book, I was watching a video of *And God Created Woman* with my wife and about halfway through I commented, uncontroversially, as I thought: 'You've got to admit that she's attractive.' She turned to me and responded acidly: 'I feel very alienated from you.' She explained that she felt excluded by Bardot on screen, as if she was not intended for her, or for any woman. In the film's story, such as it is, Bardot's relationships with other women are aggressively defiant, but also fundamentally trivial and unheeding. She directs her serious attention to the male character, enticing, exploiting and rejecting. In the same way, my wife argued, as an actress she excluded half of the audience.

This can be put even more harshly. The films that followed the extraordinary international success of *And God Created Woman*, however apparently trivial or light-hearted or old-fashioned in their morality, all had the same undercurrent, embodied in Bardot's insolent sexuality, her pouting expression, her insouciant, lolling gait. She became a symbol of natural, unfettered sexuality, but though captivating it was far from benign.

This is a perennial subject in Western art. Sex is at the heart of any society, because it brings us together into couples and families and perpetuates us. Yet the sexual impulse in its single-mindedness and self-gratification is also the great destroyer of communities. Brigitte Bardot was one of the first representatives of a whole new culture that was based on the individualistic notion of sex, in which the pleasure outweighed notions of commitment, and in which the biological imperatives and social obligations were to be circumvented or ignored. Admittedly there had been figures in Western culture who had adopted this credo before, such as Mozart's *Don Giovanni* – and look at what had happened to him. But where Mozart's rake was dragged off to burn in hell, Brigitte Bardot was seen in magazines round the world roasting contentedly on the beach in front of her Saint-Tropez home. She embodied – all too visibly – a youthful sexual arrogance, an arrogance that was all the more shocking for being justified. If anything, her affronting self-assertion was addressed more to women than to men: I can have any man I want, she seemed to say, and any other qualities, all *your* qualities – intelligence, charm, humour, ties of affection or duty – are useless. She demonstrated in her films, whatever their ostensible morality, that there was nothing egalitarian or benign about the sexual impulse.

LEFT

The tousled look which was to influence a generation of female film stars

Compared with Bardot, permed, made-up actresses like Marilyn Monroe or Jayne Mansfield looked like industrial products. Yet Bardot's naturalness was exceedingly hard to copy for anybody except the very young, slim and beautiful – or rich. This supposed liberation from the tyranny of Hollywood's constraints itself depended on meticulous hair colouring and arranging, sunbathing and clothes, a slim figure and large, self-supporting breasts.

It had always been tacitly agreed between Hollywood and its audience, that the world portrayed in its films was an indulgent fantasy. The great Hollywood femmes fatales – Rita Hayworth in *Gilda*, Marlene

Dietrich in *Shanghai Express* — ended up apologizing and saying that they didn't really mean it. What they really wanted was to settle down and become a good wife. Like Charlie Chaplin, placed by chance at the front of a protest march in the famous scene from *Modern Times*, Brigitte Bardot suddenly found herself brandishing a banner on behalf of a new generation. The results were dismaying for her audience and no less of a challenge to Bardot. After portraying the free spirit in *And God Created Woman*, she was expected — she expected herself — to play the part in real life as well.

She quickly found that her fame was only tangentially connected to the film roles that she took. I would suspect that of those in the English-speaking world who have heard of her, not more than one in ten would be able to name a single film in which she had appeared. And not more than one in a hundred would be able to name a second film. Bardot became famous, above all, for her look, the straightish but tousled, apparently sunbleached long hair, which spread in the early sixties to other leading actresses and then by the early seventies to almost everybody. She also became known for a way of life that was associated with the sunshine of the Mediterranean and, in particular, with the small fishing village of Saint-Tropez, that she had visited ever since she was a child. By the early seventies a poster advertising vodka would indicate how synonymous the place had become with a certain lifestyle, stating: 'I thought St Tropez was a Spanish monk until I discovered Smirnoff.'

Various political and social philosophies were associated with Bardot, usually by other people, but the central one was more an impulse than a philosophy, the feeling of immortality and invulnerability that young people possess.

Perhaps the young have always felt it, but in the fifties, with their new spending power, they created their own culture to celebrate it in songs about girls, cars and summer. It is a sociological curiosity that France has never produced an international rock star of any significance whatsoever. But it did produce a prototype female for the new liberated era. The California Girls with their 'French bikinis' and their tans would never have existed in anything like the form in which they were celebrated by the Beach Boys were it not for Brigitte Bardot. Her influence was quick and vast. In his 1962 song, 'I Shall Be Free', Bob Dylan imagines President Kennedy demanding of him: 'My friend, Bob, what do we need to make the country grow?' to which Dylan replies, 'My friend, John, Brigitte Bardot.'

When he was a film critic, Graham Greene observed (in a review of a Shirley Temple movie) that a child star is a wasting asset. The same was true of an actress whose appeal was based on untamed youthfulness, and indeed of a culture founded on summer holidays, proms and dates. Bardot was to be partly a victim of her own success. When everybody has come to look like Brigitte Bardot, then Brigitte Bardot has come to look like everybody. Like most actresses she would also be a victim of time, not least because she was identified with a perishable way of life, and all the more so because of the intense spotlight of media attention that was focused on it because of her. When Gilbert Adair produced *Myths and Memories*, his own thoroughly English answer to Georges Perec's *Je me souviens*, memory number 362 was: 'I remember when the French Riviera seemed to me impossibly glamorous and inaccessible.' The amusement and poignancy of this resides in our shared sense of how

Bardot embodied natural spontaneity — and the cameras were generally there to reward it

quickly the French Mediterranean has become tawdry, overrun by crowds wishing to share in the glamorous existence that Bardot, among others, revealed to us. In 1989 Bardot announced that she was leaving Saint-Tropez. She was already disgusted by the filth, the pollution, the tourists, the homosexuals, and then, as a final insult, the local council banned dogs from the village's beach. The local mayor, Alain Spada responded robustly: 'Sure, Saint-Tropez is a dying village, but who attracted the vice and shamelessness here?'

Such charges were nothing new. Simone de Beauvoir described how, in 1959, three teenagers from the French city of Angers had been arrested for the murder of an elderly man who had fallen asleep on a train. A local parent-teacher's association denounced Bardot to the city's deputy-mayor. It was she, they claimed, who was really guilty of the crime. *And God Created Woman* had been shown in Angers and the local young people had been perverted.

Yet such strictures were the worst threat that Bardot faced and her guilt-free hedonism, to the extent that it was guilt-free, and to the extent that it was enjoyable, now seems to belong to another epoch altogether. From the vantage point of the nineties, even Bardot's sun-bathing in the intense Mediterranean sun looks like a high-risk activity, and today we read of her edenically joyous, serial sex life in much the same wistful spirit that we see Paul Henreid and Bette Davis lighting cigarettes in *Now Voyager* or William Powell and Myrna Loy lining martinis along the bar in *The Thin Man*.

RIGHT

Bardot, the inhabitant of a lost, sun-drenched Mediterranean Eden

OVERLEAF

The first actress to demonstrate that sexual pleasure could be a way of life

Generations of beautiful actresses have been forgotten as they entered middle age and we have continued to think of them solely as they survived on the screen in their past films. The growing old of Brigitte Bardot has always been something different. Each year the newspapers have marked her birthdays, as if in disbelief, with feeble jokes about the sex kitten who (at fifty) 'is now a shy and retiring tabby' or (at fifty-five) 'no more a pathetic, ageing kitten, more a seasoned tigress'. She

somehow remains in the public mind, much against her will, as a first love or sexual experience, as she was when first encountered, the triumphantly defiant adolescent.

America had produced Marlon Brando, James Dean and Elvis Presley but it was as if the culture couldn't come up with an equivalent woman. Bardot expressed their rebelliousness in a different way. In her first years of fame in the fifties, she lacked their sense of tragedy, of self-pity. She suggested that sexual pleasure could be a way of life, and in some of her films we saw glimpses – often cruelly truncated by censors – of what this might be like. In the decade that followed this was put into practice, in privileged sections of the Western world, and in Bardot's own life. In the 1970s she retired from the cinema and from much of human society: 'I hate humanity – I am allergic to it ... I see no one. I don't go out. I am disgusted with everything. Men are beasts, and even beasts don't behave as they do.'

Bébé

Many women have endured terrible things in order to become film stars. There was the notorious economic and sexual exploitation from which even child stars like Shirley Temple had to protect themselves. Actresses who were being groomed for stardom would be rigorously tutored in acting and dance, rechristened with a suitably Anglo-Saxon name (Elisabeth Grasle becoming Betty Grable, Lucille Le Sueur becoming Joan Crawford) and then even physically remade to conform to some platonic ideal. Marlene Dietrich had her back teeth extracted in order to tighten the skin over, and hence accentuate, her cheekbones. Rita Hayworth, though neurotically squeamish about any sort of pain, was compelled to have her hairline shifted back by a full inch – each hair being removed and root killed with a small electric shock – in order to make her less oppressively Latinate in appearance. The face cream applied to Dolores Costello was so ferocious that it literally corroded her cheeks. Other actresses went bald because of the strength of the bleach applied to their hair year after year. It was taken for granted that women would do anything in order to have their chance of stardom, or, if nothing else, of bit-partdom.

Bardot was never driven in this way. In retirement she has repeatedly insisted that she was never much interested in the cinema even at the height of her career and that now she doesn't care at all. In 1958, when she was the most famous film star in the world, she professed a complete lack of ambition: 'I want to lie in the sun,' she complained to one interviewer, 'and do nothing and be quiet.' The great American film stars fought for stardom as an escape from poverty and obscurity. By contrast, careers as a model, a theatre actress, a film star, a world famous sex symbol, were each offered to a reluctant Bardot on a succession of plates and accepted with a pout, then rejected when the mood took her.

It was a matter of class. Bardot was born on 28 September 1934 to a wealthy middle-class family. Her father, Louis, known in the family as Pilou, was the president and managing director of a firm whose factory in northern Paris manufactured liquid oxygen. She and her younger sister, Marie-Jeanne (known as Mijanou), grew up in a prosperous, stable environment in the fifteenth and then the sixteenth arrondissment in central Paris, spending weekends at their grandmother's house near Versailles and summers in Biarritz or in Saint-Tropez. This tripartite residential arrangement has been the structure for most of her life.

Brigitte attended a prestigious private school and a surviving school photograph shows her wearing wire-framed glasses much like her father's. When the adult Bardot looked back in order to trace the reasons for her rebellion against the respectable values represented by her parents she recalled just one significant breach in the family. After some forgotten offence, her parents had forbidden the nine-year-old Brigitte and her five-year-old sister ever again to address them using the familiar *tu*. She claimed that this had left her feeling like an orphan.

LEFT

The young Brigitte (left), with a friend

Brigitte showed no significant academic promise and was interested only in ballet. Roger Vadim has recalled that when he met Bardot, her ambition was to become a ballerina. Her parents hoped she would marry a banker, an industrialist, or, failing that, a diplomat or an engineer. But her alliterative name, as well as the encouragement in her training in the performing arts, suggests at least a hint of vicarious ambition on the part of Brigitte's mother, Anne-Marie (familiarly known as Toti). In 1934 the name would have been particularly reminiscent of the film star, Simone Simon, who was then making her name in films directed by Marc Allégret.

Biographers, colleagues and friends have tried to inject a little spurious drama into the process by which Bardot was discovered. Glasses or not, photographs of her as an adolescent show her to be strikingly attractive. Her beauty as well as her talent were apparent to everybody who encountered her. In 1947 she was admitted to the National Conservatory of Music and Dancing and swiftly began to work as a catwalk model. Two years

OPPOSITE ————————

A rare photograph of a bespectacled Bardot, here shown at school

LEFT ————————————

Bardot's early ambition was to be a ballet dancer

later her mother was asked by a friend, Hélène Lazareff, editor-in-chief of *Elle* magazine, whether Brigitte's photograph could be used to accompany an article about the new French generation. It was a commission of prophetic genius, and was instrumental in fulfilling its own prophecy. Bardot was not discovered walking in the street, like Béatrice Dalle, or sitting at the counter in Schwab's drugstore, like Lana Turner, but in the photograph commissioned by Lazareff and used as a cover shot. Marc Allégret, who was now in his late forties and still one of France's leading film directors, decided to offer Bardot a screen test and sent his young assistant, nineteen-year-old Roger Vadim, along to see her family.

Roger Vladimir Plemiannikov was the child of Russian emigrants who had been living a semi-vagrant, bohemian existence in Saint-Germain-des-Prés. He was charming, handsome, bright, shrewd and he quickly made his way in that singular culture. As Vadim himself — an unashamed namedropper — put it baldly, he was friends with obscure young people and 'already famous people such as Jean Cocteau, Jacques Prévert, Boris Vian, Jean Genet, and assorted stage and screen stars. I also knew Colette, Edith Piaf, Maurice Chevalier, Jean-Paul Sartre, Albert Camus, André Gide, Salvador Dali and some great jazz musicians.' (There is something poignant about a man who spent his teenage years with people of this calibre and has spent his fifties, and now his sixties, hawking dubious properties to Hollywood producers who can only vaguely have heard of him or, indeed, most of the names on the above list.)

Vadim caught the eye of Marc Allégret, who not only employed him as an assistant but encouraged him to write a screenplay. In Vadim's own hyperbolic words: 'I

OPPOSITE

The young Brigitte's attractiveness in front of the camera was quickly apparent

LEFT

The teenager, modelling accessories

had become the youngest screenplay writer in France. And perhaps the world.' Vadim's script, *Les Lauriers sont coupés*, was never filmed but it was for this project that Brigitte Bardot took her first screen test. Louis Bardot forbade his daughter to take a screen test just as he had forbidden her to be photographed by *Elle* but this may well have just been an act, played out in the knowledge that he would be overruled by his wife. (Both Pilou and Toti would always be proud of their daughter's success and would remain in close contact with her.) She was coached for the test by Vadim, once a week after her dancing class. The test itself was inconclusive but the more important result was that she and Vadim fell in love and began a passionate affair, carried out like a Feydeau farce under the nose of Louis Bardot who vowed to his fifteen-year-old daughter that he would shoot Vadim if the young man ever took advantage of her.

By his own account Vadim was torn between wanting to corrupt his young lover and wanting to protect her, and his behaviour towards her was a confused mixture of the two. In his lurid account of their first years together ('What bowled me over when I saw her naked was the extraordinary mixture of innocence and femininity, of immodesty and timidity' and so on and on) Vadim seems to have been constructing the scenarios that would later make the two of them notorious.

Though they were charmed by Vadim, and reassured by his employer, the urbane and cultured Allégret, this itinerant hanger-on was far from the solid bourgeois son-in-law they were looking for, and the relationship was first discouraged and then strictly policed, to no avail in either case. When she was sixteen, her parents made a last attempt to separate the couple and Brigitte respond-

ed with a serious attempt at gassing herself in the family oven. She nearly died and her parents yielded to her will. She would be allowed to marry Vadim when she was eighteen and the wedding took place on 20 December 1952. Two conditions were imposed by the resigned Pilou. The bridegroom must become a Catholic and he

ABOVE

The three photogenic Bardot women — (from the left) Toti, Mijanou and Brigitte — pose on the eve of Brigitte's marriage to Vadim. The bride's father seems unconvinced by his future son-in-law

LEFT

The bourgeois young actress was attracted to Roger Vadim's bohemian sophistication

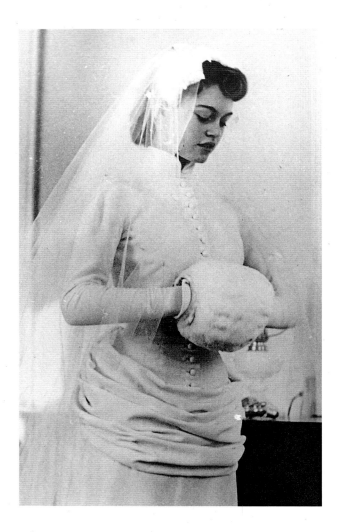

Bardot in December 1952 — demure in her role as the young bride — in her first wedding dress, later to be auctioned on behalf of animals

Fresh-faced, confident and thoroughly clothed, Bardot in her film debut, LE TROU NORMAND

must obtain proper paid employment. In the event the local priest accepted Vadim's Russian Orthodox religion and a promise that any children would be brought up in the faith in lieu of an actual Catholic baptism. An old friend secured Vadim a job as a reporter on *Paris Match*, one of the magazines that within a few years would so plague his new bride.

In the snapshot taken of the family on the day of the ceremony, Bardot, triumphantly assured, and almost eerily beautiful, seems insistently modern in contrast to the more traditional good looks of her sister and mother, who are striking enough in their own right. (Pilou looks like a frail old man, inadequate to the task of chaperoning three women who appear to be his errant granddaughters.) Brigitte was never more than an appendage to a hanger-on of the bohemian world of Paris, but she had the look to perfection, short slacks, polo neck sweater and her long brown hair swept right back. The pout, emphasized by lipstick, was fully formed.

By the time of her marriage, without any apparent effort on her part, Bardot was already more famous than her husband, and indeed the wedding attracted a fair amount of press coverage. Bardot was by now a well known face, and in fact she had already made her first film, *Le Trou normand*. French comedies have an international reputation on a level with French pop music and this rural tale of a village simpleton who inherits an inn on the condition that he returns to the local school to complete his education is not a work with any claims on anybody's time. Nevertheless, it shows precisely why Bardot had so little trouble making her way as an attractive supporting actress in minor films during the mid-fifties. She was later to be dismissive of the beginning of

her career: 'I was just a cheap little starlet hardly acting at all in a very mediocre film.' Despite Vadim's encouragement she showed no interest in attending acting classes but in her first film she reveals herself to be a competent performer, at ease in front of the camera, even with her hair tied back to hide its opulence and her breasts constrained to disguise their size.

From this she went straight to a role in one of the major French theatrical productions of the decade, the première of Jean Anouilh's *Ring Round the Moon*. It was to be the only stage performance of her career, yet she attracted favourable comment, not least from the author who was captivated by her.

Once Bardot had achieved international notoriety with her deliberately gauche performance in *And God Created Woman*, the assertion that she couldn't act became commonplace. In fact, she had already given a very accomplished performance in one of the finest French films ever made, René Clair's *Les Grandes manoeuvres (Summer Manoeuvres)*. Bardot was supporting two great actors at their best, Michèle Morgan as a middle-aged divorcée and Gérard Philipe as the rakish officer who seduces her, and she was not disgraced in their company. If she had been a little more ambitious as an actress, she might well have had a brief, minor career playing pert, beautiful young women on the stage and in prestigious films.

Vadim always insisted, with endearing modesty, that he had wrongly been accorded the credit for 'inventing' Brigitte Bardot. She did not need inventing because that was what she was really like. The British film industry

LEFT

Bardot, accomplished and appealing in René Clair's masterpiece, LES GRANDES MANOEUVRES, 1955

279-58

received a hint of this when, virtually as a matter of chance, she was hired to play opposite Dirk Bogarde in *Doctor at Sea*.

Britain in 1955 was a grey, austere place in which post-war rationing had only just been brought to an end. Bardot entered England, an unfathomable import to the bleak land of Morris Minors and Norman Wisdom. Much like those fabled first glimpses of a Coca-Cola bottle after the war that the deprived Britons didn't quite know what to make of, Bardot was a baffling example of unfettered sex. When she was due to appear in the film's mandatory 'comic' shower scene, the apparently nude body glimpsed in silhouette through the shower curtain, she appalled the British technicians by strolling naked across the set. The director, Ralph Thomas, who would later direct *Percy*, a nudge-nudge comedy about a penis transplant, was dismayed by his star's behaviour: 'I found her an excessively frank girl. And she was very proud of her body.'

The British proved easy to shock. At a press conference she was asked which had been the most memorable day of her life: 'It was a night,' was her reply. She received wide coverage and was termed a 'sex-kitten' an expression which the British press applied to her.

Bardot's co-star, Dirk Bogarde, was more impressed and instantly saw her significance, and the limitations of a British cinema in which he himself would never be content: 'Even without a French accent, Brigitte would be too much for British studios to handle. You see, Brigitte takes the trouble to put across sex as an art. With many of our girls, it's farce.'

And Vadim
Created Bardot

It had quickly been appreciated that there was something special about Brigitte Bardot. But what could be done with her in the staid, highly traditional French cinema? By the archaically repressive standards that prevailed in Britain, France seemed almost inconceivably advanced in sexual matters. Indeed the British Censors tolerated a sexual frankness in imported French films that was not permitted in domestic products because of the assumption that this was how the British expected the French to behave, though even with this dispensation the constraints remained severe.

Nevertheless, though freer than elsewhere, the treatment of sex in France was in its own way both circumscribed and formulaic. A typical example was the comedy, *En effeuillant la marguerite* (translated as *Plucking the Daisy* or, more regrettably, as *Please Mr Balzac*, or ludicrously, in Britain, as *Mam'zelle Striptease*), directed by Marc Allégret and written by Roger Vadim, who was now on extended leave from *Paris Match*. Bardot stars as Agnès, a young girl who has improbably written a scandalous, though pseudonymous, bestselling book about her own life in a provincial town, made worse because her father, a general, is one of the most respected local figures. She runs away to Paris where she meets and falls in love with a charismatic journalist. In order to raise money in an emergency, she enters a striptease competition which she wins, her identity protected by a mask and a further pseudonym. However, her lover is commissioned to write a story on the stripper and becomes attracted to her. The uncontainable Bardot spirit is nullified by being split into symbolic pieces – the rebellious writer, the enticing body – and Vadim travesties the theme of sexual obsession (which somewhere, deep inside, is the germ of this idea) by turning it into a trivial comedy about misunderstanding between the sexes. An evasive, half-hearted attempt at modernity, it embodied all that was wrong with the tired traditionalism that still dominated much of the French film world. When François Truffaut saw it, years later, he reported to a colleague that it was 'so awful that it had us down in the dumps for twenty-four hours'.

Compared with the years of courtship, covert assignations and anticipation, the actual marriage between Bardot and Vadim was a disappointment. Bardot had been enticed by Vadim's bohemianism as an escape from the bourgeois respectability of her parents, but she enjoyed it less when it became a way of life. Vadim continued to live the life of an unworldly creative artist and even though the couple were presented with an elegant flat he didn't bother with the practical details of furnishing it or installing a telephone. His wife, by contrast, eagerly assumed at least the role of a housewife, travelling extravagantly around Paris by taxi in search of household bargains that might save a few *sous*.

Yet there was a part of Vadim that was not entirely free from old-fashioned bourgeois values. He would

Despite appearances, in EN
EFFEUILLANT LA MARGUERITE
(1956), Bardot played a
stripper who kept her
clothes on

always be ambivalent about the inequality of their status. His beautiful wife was already a sex symbol of sorts. She had even been offered a contract by Warner Brothers with a temptingly large salary but at the last moment she cancelled it when she contemplated the prospect of giving up her life in France for an uncertain new career in Hollywood. She would always be stubbornly resistant to leaving France, even for brief periods of lucrative work. Bardot's apparent wilfulness would frequently be indistinguishable from shrewd calculation. In Hollywood she might conceivably have become the new Greta Garbo or Ingrid Bergman, but her English was far inferior to theirs and she was more likely to have ended up as the latest Anna Sten, or any other of the failed European imports who washed up on the American West Coast, their Hollywood careers ruined and with nothing to go back to in Europe.

Even without Hollywood stardom, Bardot was already much better known than her husband. He put up with this, travelling to Rome with her when she obtained a supporting role in the international production, *Helen of Troy*, but he was tired of being known as Monsieur Bardot. Aged only twenty-six he was already a successful young screenwriter, but there seemed no prospect of achieving his real ambition, which was to direct. As he recalled grimly, in the French cinema of the mid-fifties 'youth was not a marketable commodity.'

In 1955 Vadim met a young producer, Raoul Lévy, whose ambitions were being equally thwarted by the conservatism of the system. Together they began to work on an unprecedented project, developed in an almost improvised fashion. Before they had found a story, let alone written a script, they announced that the star would be Brigitte Bardot and that it would be shot in the South of France in CinemaScope and colour, a form that was considered garish and aesthetically inferior by many French filmmakers. (Years later, Nestor Almendros, the leading cinematographer of the French New Wave movement would speak for many when he asserted that visual bad taste was impossible in black and white.) On the look-out for potential scandal, Lévy found a news item about a crime involving three brothers and a beautiful woman, which Vadim used as the basis for his story.

Classical French cinema, both at its finest — in the masterpieces of Marcel Carné and René Clair — and in the more lacklustre films of Allégret, was founded on meticulous, highly literary, almost theatrical scripts. Vadim was far more casual. When Curt Jurgens, then a successful film actor both in America and Europe, showed a kindly interest in this unorthodox young writer and producer, Vadim hastily rewrote his script to include a rich middle-aged businessman. Jurgens accepted the role partly because he was intrigued by this beautiful young actress, and Vadim, as much an opportunist as an artist, incorporated this ambiguous attraction, this captivated, voyeuristic interest, into Jurgens' role.

The plot of *And God Created Woman* is both rudimentary and incoherent. Bardot plays Juliette, a teenage waif temporarily released from the custody of an orphanage, on condition of good behaviour, into the protection of a respectable household in the village of Saint-Tropez where she helps out in a shop. She attracts various local men and on a whim singles out and marries a retiring young man (played by Jean-Louis Trintignant), one of

OPPOSITE

Roger Vadim looks on as his wife assumes the role of a housewife

three brothers who work as boat builders. Quickly bored, she seduces another of the brothers and publicly humiliates her husband by drinking and then dancing the mambo in public with a group of black musicians. In the end her husband wins her back and cowes Juliette by slapping her, though the world-weary, more experienced Jurgens predicts that she is a woman who will never be tamed and will always torment men.

By the orthodox standards that prevailed at the time, *And God Created Woman* was as shocking for its technical incompetence as for its modern morality. Vadim took no trouble, either as director or writer, to establish his characters. Some, like Jurgens' businessman or the local women who disapprove of Juliette, are based on familiar stereotypes, the others, the leading men, are casually observed rather than 'created'. Vadim had no time, or talent, for the detail of context or character. Though the film was substantially responsible for establishing the fame of Saint-Tropez, the film gives no sense of a society in which the characters exist. There is nothing in the background, or beyond the frame. For directors like Allégret, the film must have confirmed all his suspicions about the lack of discipline of unschooled young filmmakers and such reservations were widely shared in France where the film proved to be a financial failure.

And God Created Woman has come in later years to resemble the films it was superceding, just as the earliest automobiles now look as if they were designed to be pulled by a horse. Vadim's notorious portrait of erotic liberation can look all too like an old-fashioned, retributive moral tale, bleakly asserting sexual orthodoxy. As

Simone de Beauvoir shrewdly observed, the ostensible moral of the film was an old sexist cliché, designed to flatter masculine vanity and reassure women. If women like Juliette have gone astray it is because they are victims of society, 'because no one has ever shown them the right path, but a man, a real man, can lead them back to it.' If your wife commits adultery and dances with black men, just give her a firm clout and that will restore her to chastened decency. In the final shot of *And God Created Woman* we see a docile, adoring, humbled Bardot following Trintignant into the family home which, we infer, she is about to clean and cook for and fill with children. 'A man must be strong with Brigitte,' Vadim later said. 'It is a fact, she has not had a strong man since me.'

This interpretation of the film is accurate and of some significance, yet, as Beauvoir added, it also entirely obscures what is important about it. Certainly the point was not lost by the brilliant young cineastes like François Truffaut and Jean-Luc Godard who were then establishing their reputations as film critics. They saw a film that was made independently for very little money, shot almost entirely on location, that dispensed with orthodox structure and consistency in favour of individual obsession. The first-time director was making a virtue out of necessity because on the occasions where he attempts even briefly a sequence of straightforward narrative, the results are dismal. The sequence in which Bardot pilots a boat, which then catches fire and explodes – all in order that she may be rendered stimulatingly wet and brought together with Christian Marquand – is shamefully clumsy in its execution. Fortunately the slack construction was essential to the film's true subject. Vadim, the eternal assistant, had

briefly worked as a secretary to André Gide, and Juliette, in her aberrant unpredictability, was a character that owed more to the world of Gide, Sartre and Camus in modern literature than to the contemporary French cinema, though she arguably had even more in common with the guilt-free sexuality and maundering self-indulgence of the teenage heroine of Françoise Sagan's *Bonjour Tristesse* (published just a couple of years earlier) than the more uncompromising existential isolation of Camus' or Sartre's heroes. There was nothing troublingly radical about Vadim's style, none of the jump cuts, with which Godard would soon disconcert French filmgoers. *And God Created Woman* had a reassuring gloss deriving as much from Vadim's experience on *Paris Match* as from his association with Allégret.

Above all, the film was about Brigitte Bardot and Vadim's decisive achievement was to express on screen his own unresolved feelings about his wife. Bardot was later to recall of her first marriage: 'Whenever I walked, undressed or ate breakfast, I always had the impression he was looking at me with someone else's eyes — and with everyone's dream.'

In accounts of his liaisons with Brigitte Bardot, Catherine Deneuve and Jane Fonda — in each case before they had become major stars — Vadim has frequently been described as a Svengali, but a more appropriate comparison would be with Frankenstein, creating a new creature that then escapes his control. Vadim deserves much of the credit, or the blame, for making Brigitte Bardot what she was. He 'revealed me to myself' as she later put it. As he wrote *And God Created Woman* he deliberately made use of her own language and behaviour, often inserting her words straight into the script, offer-

ing a role that was, as he put it, 'a perfect marriage between a fictional character and the person she was in real life.' He saw his wife as a woman without a sense of sin, innocently erotic, whose sexuality was untrammelled by psychological hang-ups. If she was torn it was between her instinctive fidelity and her sexual impulsiveness. There were similar conflicts in her social attitudes. She was 'attached to bourgeois values — thrift, fear of adventure, preference for modest-size dwellings, a definite taste for ornate furniture and knick-knacks'. At the same time she was 'ahead of her time, independent to the point of scandalizing France and five continents.' Vadim's capacity to portray this objectively sounds like a model of directorial control, yet such power as the film still has derives from his capacity to dramatize his own helplessness and humiliation. Bardot may be guiltless but what about the men who watch her, the characters in the film, Vadim — the husband and director? What about us, the audience?

OPPOSITE

Bardot, Jean-Louis Trintignant and Vadim during the shooting of AND GOD CREATED WOMAN

By the time he came to work on the script, his wife had already been unfaithful to him for the first time and it was clear that the marriage was over. Then, almost as soon as shooting started, Bardot began a flagrant affair with her co-star, Jean-Louis Trintignant. Vadim could have abandoned the film, or at least forced the two lovers to stay apart. At first he insisted that at least the appearance of normality should be maintained so long as shooting continued but he swiftly saw that even that was impossible and he allowed the couple to move in together. Worse than this, as far as his own self-respect was concerned, much of the film's scandalous reputation derived from anecdotes about the confusion between illusion and reality during shooting. It was breathlessly reported, and painstakingly not denied, that the bedroom love scenes between Bardot and Trintignant had continued after Vadim called for a cut.

Aided by the intensity of his own feelings, Vadim's film became an obsessive, garbled fantasy about his receding wife. As Simone de Beauvoir put it, the world is entirely absent from Vadim's story: 'Against a background of fake colours he flashes a number of "high spots" in which all the sensuality of the film is concentrated: a strip-tease, passionate love-making, a mambo sequence.' And this discontinuity was itself a crucial part of the film's unexpected force. The audience is never allowed to be carried away by the story, it does not identify with the characters, belief is not suspended. Even the voyeuristic element of the film is paradoxical because, in her words, 'it is no fun to witness a hot performance cold-bloodedly.' In retrospect it is possible to say, as Beauvoir couldn't, that the icy voyeurism is Vadim's own. He had been a voyeur even within the privacy of the marriage and now he really was contemplating the infidelity of his wife, on set, through the lens and in reality. Beauvoir did argue, however, that in the film's notorious set-pieces, such as the climactic mambo, no member of the audience believes in the character of Juliette for a moment: 'It is BB who is exhibiting herself. She is as alone on the screen as the strip-tease artist is alone on the stage. She offers herself directly to each spectator. But the offer is deceptive, for as the spectators watch her, they are fully aware that this beautiful young woman is famous, rich, adulated and completely inaccessible.'

OPPOSITE

Bardot, Trintignant and a carefully arranged sheet in AND GOD CREATED WOMAN

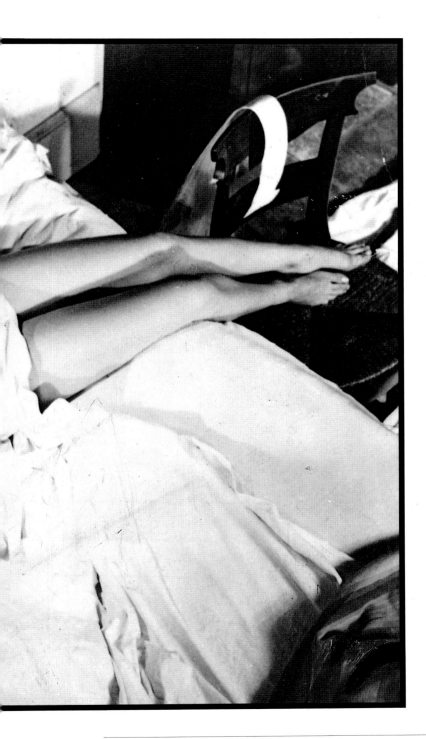

Much the same can be said of Brigitte Bardot's performance as of the film. Deprived of the experienced guidance of a director like Clair or Allégret, she lacks the polish and assurance she had brought to the delivery of her lines even in her very first film, *Le Trou normand*. Vadim handles her like a still photographer, beautifully posed and arranged. In scenes involving routine movement or substantial dialogue, much of which is clumsily written, she seems gauchely adrift. Yet even this appears part of the film's rough appeal, as if the craft of acting itself were an inhibition, another form of the etiquette imposed by respectable society which she had to throw off in order to reach some Rousseauesque liberty beyond. Skill would have been inappropriate.

Sex, in all its art and artifice, had always been one of the central themes of the cinema and even in the French cinema of 1956 nudity was scarcely unprecedented. What was startling in *And God Created Woman* was its casual disregard – which was patently Bardot's own disregard – for the evasions and disguises that traditionally accompanied screen sex. Our first glimpse of Bardot is of the outline of her naked body, golden against the white of a sheet flapping on the washing line in the bright midday sun. Vadim is all too conscious of the connection with Eve and he immediately has Curt Jurgens talk tiresomely of offering her an apple so that we don't miss the point either, but Bardot herself is supremely insouciant. There is no suspense or teasing about her nude scenes. On its release *And God Created Women* was infamously notorious worldwide for its portrayal of passionate sex but it now seems best when showing the casual behaviour of lovers, naked people wrapped in a crumpled sheet.

Bardot's nudity is brazen nakedness, and sexual

desire manifests itself as simple appetite. The best scene in the film, and by far the most erotic, is one of the few that censors were unable to get at, unless they simply banned the film entirely, which many did. On the night of the marriage, Juliette foregoes the wedding supper and simply takes her new husband upstairs leaving the respectable older people to nibble disconsolately at the

An insouciant Bardot preparing for her first appearance in
AND GOD CREATED WOMAN

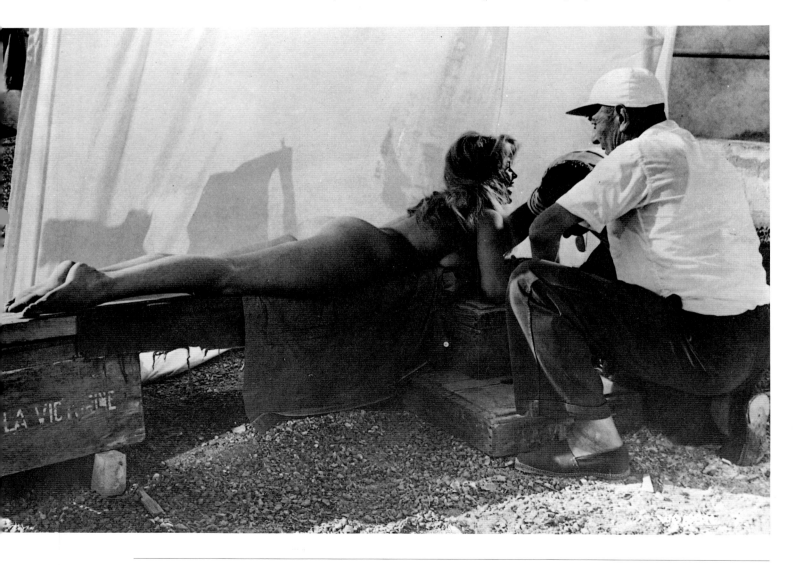

food down in the living room. Then, wearing only a dressing gown, Bardot (it seems quite wrong to refer to the character here, instead of the actress) saunters downstairs and makes her way around the table, silently taunting the stony-faced guests, helping herself to the food and a bottle of wine before returning to the marital bed. 'Does he want anything?' a woman feebly asks. 'I'll take care of him,' Bardot replies. This is sex as an anarchic force which is uncontainable within the rituals and ceremonies that society has invented to channel and limit it.

This, the character of Bardot as Juliette, would also inspire the young directors of the new wave, with the portraits of wayward, determined young women who stalk through their films. In the early sixties, the distinguished American critic, Dwight Macdonald, asked François Truffaut about the puzzling character of Catherine, the heroine of *Jules et Jim*, played by Jeanne Moreau. Truffaut replied: 'She is a woman who wants to live like a man because that is her nature. The people in my film reject conventional morality, but they have their own kind, a higher one and an absolute one.'

What remains disconcerting about *And God Created Woman* is that Juliette articulates no protest or resentment. There is no case to be answered or argument to be countered. She just takes what she wants. She does not so much defy traditional morality as pass it by without noticing it. Writing as early as 1959, Beauvoir, the most influential feminist writer of her time, sensed the radical social implications of Bardot's intuitive behaviour. Men were comfortable with women who could be flirted with, whose bottoms could be pinched: 'A ribald gesture reduces a woman to a thing that a man can do with as he pleases without worrying about what goes on in her

mind and heart and body.' Bardot had dispensed with all these degrading rituals between the sexes, the games that had grown up around love and eroticism: 'As soon as a single myth is touched, all myths are in danger. A sincere gaze, however limited its range, is a fire that may spread and reduce to ashes all the shoddy disguises that camouflage reality.' Startlingly original as ever, Beauvoir was hailing Bardot as an exemplar of post-feminism before most people had heard of feminism.

The Bardot of *And God Created Woman*, startled audiences with the unconventionality not just of her behaviour but of her appearance. The hair had been dyed and brushed out, falling across her shoulders and down her back in natural splendour. The sunbathing, of which she does so much in the film and which was always to be her principal leisure activity, had turned her skin a honey brown colour. In her films made a year or two earlier she looked like a pert forties' bit part actress (or in the case of *Les Grandes manoeuvres*, a pert nineteenth-century stage actress), but here she suddenly looks as if she has stepped back from the sixties or even the early seventies. As people sensed, with excitement or horror, Bardot was a hint of something that was coming, a politics that was based on pleasure and gratification, the replacement of manners with instinct, of exterior duty with inner compulsion, of the fifties with the sixties.

But it cannot be left there, on that triumphantly anticipatory note. Beauvoir's essay was titled 'Brigitte Bardot and the Lolita Syndrome' and she was aware that in sexual matters there was no such thing as a simple step forward. If one form of stimulation had been abolished, others would have to be invented and among the more dubious attributes of Juliette are her youth and

innocence. If adult men and women had been brought together, then the exciting gap could be re-established by transferring attention to younger girls: 'At least that is what those who have created a new Eve by merging the "green fruit" and *"femme fatale"* types have pinned their hopes on.'

Bardot was a twenty-two-year-old impersonating a virgin teenager. Her attitude to sex may have been uncomplicated but the same could not be said of Vadim, who was preoccupied with the fifteen-year-old girl he had first met, the unknown whom he had made famous, the virgin who was intuitively skilled at lovemaking, the blank slate for others to write on, the innocent who caused chaos in a corrupt world. Vadim constantly cited the Eden myth in attempting to describe Bardot, but he had no interest in the Fall as a religious event, concerned with sin and temptation. For him the only way it could be expressed was in the innocence of the child. Like Eve, Juliette's sexual desire is just another impulse, like gluttony or narcissism, because she is unsocialized and untrained. Far from being liberating, Vadim's portrayal of unfettered impulse was just another stereotype.

The retreat to instinct, the escape from society, is always a paradoxical enterprise. Robinson Crusoe, alone on his island, recreates in miniature the rational, ordered world he has left behind, and when he meets one other man, he colonizes him. After all the humiliations and affronts, how does Juliette finally goad her husband into striking her and seizing control of the marriage? She dances the mambo in a club with a group of African musicians. Vadim, the radical liberator, makes use of one of the most primal racist symbols, the idea that the sexuality of 'our' white women might be roused and exploited by the potent black man.

Vadim's opportunistic use of this motif in 1956 verges on the inflammatory. France had just lost a colonial war in Indo-China, with the humiliating defeat in Dien-Bien-Phu and the subsequent withdrawal of French forces from Vietnam. This had been followed almost immediately by a revolt in Algeria, then considered to be an integral part of France. The Socialist prime minister, Guy Mollet, took office in 1956 with the intention of negotiating with the rebels but under pressure from French residents in Algeria he reversed his position and embarked on a bloody and entirely futile wave of repression, attempting to smash the Algerian nationalists. The French army drew heavily on conscripts and every young Frenchman faced the possibility of having to fight to keep Algeria French. It was in this context of anti-colonialist revolt that Bardot tormented her weak husband by flirting with an African.

The scene is scarcely less unsettling today, with Bardot married to a leading politician of an anti-immigrant political party, and closely identified with the South of France where she still spends a great deal of her time, an area notorious for its preoccupation with the issues of race and immigration. Yet even this shallow bigotry can be taken as a further example of Brigitte Bardot's uncompromising power, embodying the untrammelled sexual instinct in all its enticing excitement, but also its unheeding cruelty and its perversity, its forbidden fantasies. If she had started a revolution, she took no responsibility for where it would lead.

OPPOSITE _____

Sex, race and jealousy: Bardot dances the mamba in front of Jean-Louis Trintignant at the climax of AND GOD CREATED WOMAN

After the Creation

And God Created Woman, which had been poorly reviewed and financially unsuccessful on its home territory, took an extraordinary four million dollars on its first release in America, and was an equal *succès de scandale* in many countries across the world, from Britain to Japan. The film was often heavily cut and re-edited, with any suggestion of sex or nudity, let alone the sex or nudity itself, removed. In certain scenes, such as the sex scene beneath an oppressively phallic tree on the beach, Vadim had prudently shot two different versions, with his wife clothed and naked (the tree remained identically tumescent in both versions). Whatever was cut, Bardot remained present in some form or another and her voracious erotic presence was as obvious in scenes where she nibbled on a carrot, helped herself to food from the wedding feast or danced the mambo, as it was in the more obviously shocking sex scenes. Even where she appears clothed, her garb frequently seems like a temporary expedient, only emphasizing the naked body beneath. For the majority of audiences, even a watered-down or cut Bardot was far more shocking in what was taken for granted about the sexual consciousness of a young girl than anything they had been permitted to see before. As the distinguished American critic, Hollis Alpert, observed: 'She sets men dreaming of a no-holds-barred encounter with her.'

Bardot's own status was unparalleled. A profile of her in the *Daily Mail* would state as an obvious fact that she was the 'one actress who can claim universal appeal … a boost to the box-offices of the entire world.' It had never happened before and will never happen again. An actress had eclipsed Hollywood stars like Marilyn Monroe and Audrey Hepburn because of her success in a single independent film made in France. This achievement was abetted by a crisis in the American film industry, which had been gravely weakened by the rise of television and the collapse of the studio system. Once again, Brigitte Bardot was unintentionally showing the way forward. During the fifties, Hollywood had desperately searched for something it could give audiences that television couldn't, such as vast wide screens or gimmicks like 3D. None was more than briefly profitable. The success of *And God Created Woman* suggested other possibilities. The major television networks were, as they still are, tightly constrained by their family audience and their advertisers, and could not hope to compete with cinemas in the coverage of adult themes of sex, violence, drugs and so-called 'bad' language. Hollywood actresses would soon look like Brigitte Bardot, with their carefully styled natural long hair, and most of them would also be shedding their clothes like Brigitte Bardot, getting in or out of bed and wrapping themselves in the sheets, swimming, showering, entangling their limbs with those of their co-star. In practice the ways of providing glimpses of the naked human body on screen are limited and Bardot had demonstrated most of them.

Bardot was a new kind of film star. No filmgoer ever felt intimate with Marlene Dietrich any more than any

ABOVE

AND GOD CREATED WOMAN: Bardot, Christian
Marquand and a tumescent tree

tourist felt intimate with the Statue of Liberty. They heard things about Marilyn Monroe and perhaps thought they glimpsed her vulnerability through the cracks in her comic persona. But with Brigitte Bardot it was the real thing. The viewer had casually wandered into her bedroom and found her lying there unconcerned and uninhibited. She wasn't embarrassed by their presence and each could become a liberated bohemian for the ninety minutes – or however long the local censor had left them – of *And God Created Woman*.

The confusion between illusion and reality has always been a problem for actresses. Rita Hayworth once reflected sadly on her most famous role, as a provocative nightclub dancer: 'Every man I've known has fallen in love with Gilda and woken with me.' The confusion with Bardot was even more complicated because, whatever the truth, it was a major part of her appeal and she, along with Vadim, encouraged the illusion of intimacy. 'Bardot does not act, she is,' said Vadim. 'I like making sexy films. That is how I am in real life,' she said to journalists. This must have been the way it seemed. Her relationship with Vadim had begun when she was still a child and the barriers had always been flimsy between the public and private lives, between the characters she portrayed and whatever was left when she was alone. Indeed, for all of her film career she was notorious for her hatred of solitude, her need to be part of a couple at the centre of a crowd, yet also free to escape – even if it was to another man, to be part of another group.

Bardot's reputation quickly transcended the actual films she made. She was a phenomenon, stared at, attracting crowds wherever she went, a subject of intense curiosity, pursued by photographers, a symbolic public figure commented on in the media. She quickly became aware that attention of this intensity could not be ignored, because the act of ignoring it would in itself be a subject of more attention. As she perceptively commented: 'If I appear at a gala, people say, "When will she stop showing off her millions!" But if I'm seen without make-up and dressed any old way because I like it and want to feel relaxed, then they say, "Is that BB? She calls herself a star. But she's really rather ugly."'

From now on the question of whether she was behaving according to her own wishes or impulses, living up to her image, creating a false persona for media consumption, or being driven by the pressure of her public role would be difficult to answer. In the wake of her success in *And God Created Woman* she began to live the life that the public expected Bardot to lead. Her relationship with Trintignant continued for a time and she was finally granted a divorce from Roger Vadim on 6 December 1957, shortly before their fifth wedding anniversary.

LEFT

Bardot: the subject of intense public curiosity

In 1958 she bought La Madrague, a beachfront house in Saint-Tropez which would become as celebrated and symbolic a residence in its own way as Buckingham Palace, and exert a similar attraction on tourists. The difference is that the crowds peering at Buckingham Palace were kept at a discreet distance by railings and ceremonial guards. La Madrague was directly on the coast and she became a source of intrusive pilgrimage, on the official route for sightseeing boats, whose guides would point out over the intercom when the star was in residence. More determined fans would make their way on to the beach itself (the ownership of which would be a subject of dispute

RIGHT

Success made Brigitte Bardot
public property

With Sacha Distel in Saint-Tropez in 1958. He was never content with his secondary role

Bardot, contemplating her image after the success of AND GOD CREATED WOMAN

Star, car and an excuse for press comments about bodywork

for decades between Bardot and the local authorities) and even force entry into the house.

In a press interview, shortly after the divorce, Vadim lamented that Bardot was on her way to becoming a neurotic: 'To be happy, Brigitte has to be in a constant state of physical excitement. Unless she is physically stimulated, lying in the sun, or swimming in the sea, or making love, or playing with animals, she is unhappy. Her trouble is that she doesn't like people.'

After the failure of the relationship with Trintignant, Bardot embarked on a string of the affairs that from then on would be more widely publicized than her films. Her most famous partner of that time was Sacha Distel, then just beginning to make his reputation as a singer. Bardot discovered that while she was free to behave like a man, few men were willing to put up for any length of time with the subordinate role of the disregarded and exploited woman, especially with the intense publicity that any aspect of Bardot's private life received. Distel was completely unwilling to sacrifice his own interests, as he later protested: 'I was working hard to become Sacha Distel, successful singer, not Mr Bardot. If Brigitte felt like it she could have been Mrs Distel. There was never any doubt in my mind that anybody I married would have to be Mrs Distel.' The problem with living the life of a liberated woman in a society that was still as patriarchal and sexist as ever was that the woman was likely to find herself as exploited and abused as any ordinary unliberated woman, but with the added frustration of being considered to deserve everything she got.

Bardot's more immediately pressing problem was her future as an actress. She was signed up to no contract, she was not part of a studio system and she was in the process of getting divorced from her mentor. She seemed free to do what she wanted. The obvious option, that had traditionally been chosen by successful European actresses, was to go to Hollywood. She had rejected a contract from Warner Brothers five years earlier but now she would be free to work on her own terms. In the wake of her international success, Vadim and Raoul Lévy conceived the idea of a collaboration with Frank Sinatra on a musical comedy to be called *Paris by Night*. Granted an entrée because of their newly secured commercial reputation, Lévy and Vadim visited Sinatra, ate, drank and went to boxing matches with him, agreed on a story

and commissioned a script. However, Bardot refused to work in Hollywood, Sinatra refused to work in Paris, and the film was never made.

Une Parisienne, Bardot's first film to be made after *And God Created Woman*, was a trivial, old fashioned comedy. She plays the daughter of the prime minister, a flighty girl who is in love with her father's principal secretary. A farcical accident compels the man to marry her to avoid a political scandal and she then wins his love by conducting a flirtation with a foreign monarch (played by Charles Boyer) who is in France on a state visit. The film is only significant in its attempt to make use of the lucrative but disturbing new Bardot persona, while defusing it and making it safe. The most famous scene in the film features Bardot and her new husband sleeping in adjacent rooms on their wedding night. Both are tormented by their mutual lust until he joins her: it's the old myth of the eager virgin who must be both tamed and satisfied by her husband. In purely commercial terms, films like *Une Parisienne*, were the best propositions for Bardot's career because they contained what might otherwise seem to be her subversive sexuality by turning it into endearing mischief.

Though separated from Roger Vadim, Bardot agreed, out of a sense of gratitude or obligation, to appear in the new film he had developed with Lévy, *Les Bijoutiers du clair de lune* (known in English as *The Night Heaven Fell* and *Heaven Fell That Night*). This was Vadim's ambitious attempt at a Hollywood-style *film noir*, about a young girl who runs

away through rural Spain with the man who has killed her wicked uncle. Vadim hired the promising young Irish actor, Stephen Boyd, for the leading role (two years later Boyd would play the villain, Messala, opposite Charlton Heston in *Ben Hur*) and recruited a skiing friend, Peter Viertel (a promising young scriptwriter who had worked on John Huston's *The African Queen*), to polish the script

OPPOSITE ——————————————————

Vadim and Bardot, back together again for LES BIJOUTIERS DU CLAIR DE LUNE *(1957)*

BELOW ——————————————————

The British poster for Bardot's first film after the infamous AND GOD CREATED WOMAN

CHARLES BOYER
HENRI VIDAL
Brigitte Bardot
Parisienne

Produced by
FRANCIS COSNE   Directed by
MICHEL BOISROND
AN ARIANE – FILMSONOR PRODUCTION
A FILMS DE FRANCE RELEASE
RANK FILM DISTRIBUTORS LTD.

The Love and Laughter story that could only happen in Paris!

ABOVE

The press quotes say it all for EN CAS DE MALHEUR (LOVE IS MY PROFESSION)

OPPOSITE

Bardot, Vadim, Stephen Boyd and a donkey that proved to be infectious, on the set of LES BIJOUTIERS DU CLAIR DE LUNE

and produce an English version which could be shot simultaneously for the foreign market. In the event, Bardot – conscious of her linguistic limitations – refused to speak the English lines. The film was shot under difficult conditions of extreme heat, exacerbated, in the case of Vadim and Lévy, by a severe pancreatic infection they contracted from a donkey that Bardot had adopted and insisted they cared for.

The film, a simple story dully and confusingly told, cruelly exposes the shortcomings of Vadim as a filmmaker. He had a sense of style and a shrewd perception of what the public expected of his star. Bardot has a shower scene, and after smouldering enticingly at Stephen Boyd for most of the film she prefaces their first sexual encounter by confessing that actually, despite her provocative behaviour, she is a virgin. In *Les Bijoutiers*, Bardot plays a younger, even less experienced character than in *And God Created Woman*. It was as if Vadim was attempting to move her back to the way she was when they first met or, more likely, as if what he found exciting about her was this transition from schoolgirl to lover and he wanted to recreate it on screen once more. What Vadim entirely lacked was a gift for narrative, even of the most straightforward linear kind.

Les Bijoutiers' limitations were exposed by Bardot's next film, *En cas de malheur* (lubriciously translated as *Love is My Profession*). Here she would be starring opposite Jean Gabin, one of the greatest of all French film actors. Before shooting he dismissed her contemptuously as 'something that strolls around in the nude' but after the film had been completed he acknowledged that she was a 'real professional'. She was already afflicted by the

publicity that surrounded her. The distinguished director, Claude Autant-Lara had been warned off but he later summed her up, in words that were meant to be kind, as 'not terrible at all. She is a nice child.'

The actress one cannot avoid comparing with Brigitte Bardot is Marilyn Monroe. They were the two great sex symbols of their time, vastly popular with the general public, yet they also fascinated intellectuals. Both worked with the major serious directors in their respective industries. In the 1950s Monroe worked with John Huston, Joseph Manckiewicz, Fritz Lang, Howard Hawks, Otto Preminger, Billy Wilder, Laurence Olivier, Joshua Logan and George Cukor, an extraordinary list of names, though the results were frequently disappointing because of the difficulty of finding the right role for her singular but limited and frail talents. There was something cartoonish and nebulous about her and she was generally most at ease in comedy when she could be artificial. No director every attempted to interrogate her unease directly, or to explore the sexual allure that is preserved in the best photographs of her.

Bardot also worked with many of the major directors in the French cinema but, for better or worse, they cast her because they were fascinated with the Bardot phenomenon, with her fame or with the new attitude to sexuality she seemed to represent. These directors approached her in much the same spirit as their literary contemporaries like Simone de Beauvoir and Marguerite Duras felt compelled to write essays exploring her character. It was only well after Monroe's death that she attracted this sort of literary attention, from writers like Norman Mailer, Angela Carter and Gloria Steinem.

One reason was that in her lifetime Monroe was

ABOVE

Bardot on a rare visit to London. The intense curiosity of passers-by made filming impossible

never taken to represent anything in social terms. While Marilyn Monroe's affairs remained on the level of gossip, Bardot's love life became a political act, dubious though that might now seem. The eight years' difference in their ages was decisive here. In the mid-fifties, when James Dean became a star in *Rebel Without a Cause*, when the first rock and roll records were being released, Marilyn Monroe was thirty, already established and as much a figure of the past as Clark Gable, her co-star in *The Misfits*. The arrival of Bardot, by contrast, coincided with the new youth movement, for which even she, it must be said, was already a little old (four years older, for example, than Natalie Wood, Dean's co-star in *Rebel Without a Cause,* though three years younger than Dean himself). The blurred line between Bardot's films and her supposedly bohemian lifestyle seemed timely also in 1957, the year that *On the Road*, Jack Kerouac's *roman à clef* about life in the Beat generation,was published. It was the era of lost youth, of self-exploration.

There is no more telling demonstration of the difference between the two actresses than their use of a similar gesture of sexual provocation. The single most famous moment in Monroe's screen career is when, accompanied by Tom Ewell in *The Seven Year Itch* (1955), she walks across the subway grating and her dress is lifted up by a gust of wind. The point, as so often with Monroe's screen character, is that she is like a child unaware of the effect she is producing on this middle-aged man, who is aghast in the face of so much temptation. But the sexuality is so cartoonish, so burlesqued as to be made safe.

There is an equivalent scene in *En cas de malheur*. In this dark tale adapted from the 1955 novel by Georges Simenon, Bardot plays a rootless young woman who makes a hopeless attempt at a jewel robbery with a friend, in the course of which she injures an old woman. She seeks the help of a distinguished barrister (played by Jean Gabin) who, with cynical aplomb, manipulates the judicial system in order to secure her acquittal. At her first meeting with Gabin, she announces that she has no money and in response to the question of how she will pay stands and raises her short dress revealing to Gabin (from the front) and to us (from behind) that she is not wearing underwear.

The difference in the attitude towards sex revealed by the two scenes is striking. *The Seven Year Itch* plays with the notion of sexual attraction and adultery but at the same time evades confronting the reality of the relationship. Monroe's jokes, the flirtation, the childish, parodic innocence were all ways of letting the men off the hook, allowing them to feel lust while pretending it was something else, something acceptable and funny. By contrast, *En cas de malheur* is bracingly honest about sexual desire. Though happily, if sexlessly, married, Gabin allows himself to become obsessed with Bardot and abandon first his professional principles, then his marriage and home, and finally the social position which we have seen delineated in such detail. Gabin gives a superb performance, entirely lacking in melodrama or self-pity. He is a man who, while remaining sympathetic and basically clear-sighted about himself and the object of his desire, still drifts helplessly into self-destruction.

Bardot is outstanding in what could have been an intolerably unsympathetic role. She is called upon to assault a helpless old woman, to be responsible for the death of another old man (the jeweller she robbed), she casually breaks up a marriage for the sake of a relation-

About to raise her dress in payment for the legal services of Jean Gabin in the masterly EN CAS DE MALHEUR *(1957)*

ship to which she is half-heartedly committed, while keeping on another disastrous liaison with a violent medical student. Following her own impulses from moment to moment, she numbly betrays everybody including, in the end, herself.

In *En cas de malheur*, Claude Autant-Lara uncompromisingly succeeds in putting Simenon's dark world on to the screen and makes intelligent use of what Roger Vadim had only been able to point his camera at in bafflement. In this film Bardot is seen to be the latest in a long line of dangerous heroines that lure men to their destruction in *film noirs*, the women played by Joan Bennett in Fritz Lang's *Scarlet Street* (1946) or by Barbara Stanwyck in Billy Wilder's *Double Indemnity* (1944). In *En cas de malheur*, a post-Sartre, post-Camus thriller, there is no normality to be lured away from. Nor does it seem quite right to say that Gabin is corrupted. With open eyes, almost with resignation, he does what he has to do, not because he believes he will find happiness, but simply because he has to do it, and he grimly accepts his fate.

OPPOSITE ———

Bardot, a besotted Jean Gabin and his bemused secretary in EN CAS DE MALHEUR

Autant-Lara makes no attempt to demonize Yvette, Bardot's character, nor does he patronize her by 'understanding' or 'explaining' her. She is intermittently attached to Gabin and willing to set up house with him, though it can never be anything more than a Genet-like charade. She and her maid play games in which they swap roles (in the novel the game is more explicitly sexual and the trio end up in bed together). Her jealous lover destroys all the clothes Gabin has bought for her yet it is no surprise when in the following scene she is in

bed with the lover once more. She drifts through a dark, violent world guided only by the whim of the moment, unaffected by experience or by any notion of stability or commitment. Pregnant and on the verge of leaving Paris with Gabin, she casually decides to visit her ex-lover with a present and then to make love with him. Others are not so free of jealousy, and in a frenzy he stabs her to death. This existential romance is, in its way, highly traditional, the story of Cressida and Carmen and all the other retributive tales of fickle women. What is new is the refusal to judge or explain.

This remarkable film demonstrates the difference between exploring ideas and merely toying with them, as Vadim had, even in *And God Created Woman*. There is a polarity in post-Enlightenment culture in the treatment of nature and instinct, which could be summarized as the opposition between Rousseau and Sade. What is the effect of throwing off the shackles of tradition and setting our instincts free? The Rousseauesque argument is that nature is intrinsically benevolent and just, and that all would be well if we yielded to the rule of our instincts. The Sadean argument is that nature is brutal and that our natural instincts include the desire to torture and destroy. The Brigitte Bardot myth swings between these two poles. At the heart of her attraction, what made her a model for so many women, was that she seemed to provide glimpses of the Rousseauesque possibility.

The Mediterranean had already been established by the post-Impressionist movement as a centre of prelapsarian, sensual pleasure. Paul Signac, the most gifted follower of Georges Seurat, had actually settled in Saint-

OPPOSITE ————

EN CAS DE MALHEUR: The dark side of sexual desire

Tropez in 1892 and he was visited there by Matisse in 1904. During the First World War Matisse settled in Nice. Then in the thirties, Picasso began, as Robert Hughes has put it, 'to mythologize himself as the Mediterranean artist.' These artists saw themselves as reviving a pagan, classical tradition of sensual pleasure. Brigitte Bardot gave this notion flesh — her own flesh — transforming this highly refined hedonism into a mass market industry. It was the democratizing of Eden that the sixties would promise: if we let our hair grow, lie in the sun and cast off our inhibitions imposed by clerics, old people and other tyrants, the result will be a Utopia of the senses. There was an ambiguity even about the artists' idealization of a Mediterranean coastline that was being destroyed in front of their eyes, and the presence of Brigitte Bardot as the principal tourist attraction of the Côte d'Azur only accelerated the process.

OPPOSITE

Pablo Picasso in 1956, contemplating various monuments to Mediterranean culture

Likewise there is always something ambiguous about Bardot's innocence, as Simone de Beauvoir noted, in response to the criticism that Bardot the actress had only one expression: 'It is true that the outer world is hardly reflected in it at all and that it does not reveal great inner disturbance. But that air of indifference becomes her. BB has not been marked by experience. Even if she has lived — as in *Love is My Profession* — the lessons that life has given her are too confused for her to have learned anything from them. She is without memory, without a past, and, thanks to this ignorance, she retains the perfect innocence that is attributed to a mythical childhood.'

This is not a benign innocence. Bardot is far more

tellingly childlike in *En cas de malheur* than in *And God Created Woman*. In the latter the childlike quality has been imposed by Vadim himself and its only purpose is as a perverse further attraction, the supposed eroticism of innocence. He has no interest in the men's motivation beyond the bland assumption that all the men – the characters in the film, Vadim himself and the male filmgoers – will collude in salivating over the beautiful creature that he is offering us. In *En cas de malheur* Autant-Lara shows us what a strange thing lust is, how separate it is from everything else about us. We are aware that Gabin himself can almost see it, tugging him away from a happy and secure life. On the other hand, Autant-Lara demonstrates the peculiarity of innocence, how close the innocent is to the psychopath. The moment when Brigitte Bardot silences the screaming woman by striking her over the head with a hammer is wonderfully funny and frightening. It would seem as appropriate to blame her for it as to imprison a child for tossing a doll, with which it had grown bored, to one side.

The perverse, role-swapping games that Bardot plays with her maid in the ménage she shares with Gabin are deeply unsettling, even in the sanitized screen version, because of the clash of worlds and imaginations. She is a form of child for whom even sex and power are objects to be toyed with and amusingly rearranged. He is embarrassed yet tolerates it because, we infer, he finds it sexually arousing. Yet this collusive game is rendered appalling by the presence and enforced participation of the young maid, nervous and glum. It is an unsparing analysis of sex and its connections to power and class. It was important to Bardot's career as well. For the first time she was recognized as a credible actress.

Lust and self-destruction: Gabin and Bardot in EN CAS DE MALHEUR

Private Lives

At the height of her fame Bardot's body was used as the model for Marianne, the statue of the spirit of the Revolution that stands in every Hôtel de ville in France. It was a hopeful way of co-opting this wayward star on behalf of respectable civic society. We want to have it both ways with our objects of desire. They stand for fantasy, for the danger and passion missing from our own lives, but in the end we want to be reassured that at heart they are just simple housewives, farmgirls, mothers. Bardot was unpopular in France for the same reason that people were obsessed with her, because of her refusal to make even the gesture of respecting ordinary pieties.

When Simone de Beauvoir came to write her essay, Bardot was in her mid-twenties and Beauvoir anticipated that she would have to remake her personality in order to win the affection of the French people. She noted, for example, that Bardot had recently spoken with enthusiasm for rural life and her dream of taking up farming and Beauvoir commented that in France 'love of cows is regarded as a token of high morality.' Furthermore, at an official lunch, Bardot had reputedly impressed the director of the Bank of France with her knowledge of finance: 'To know how to place one's money is a supreme virtue in the eyes of the French bourgeoisie.' Bardot's sexual autonomy posed a threat to traditional notions of marriage and the family and there was a popular hope that it might be renounced. When was she going to become respectable and settle down?

For conventional opinion, the year of 1959 looked promising. *Babette s'en va-t-en guerre* (*Babette Goes to War*) was a feeble comedy in which Bardot plays a spy parachuted into occupied France, but it marked an obvious attempt at a change of style, in a film that was designed – however incompetently – for a family audience. Better still she had fallen in love again, with her co-star, Jacques Charrier, and this, she announced, was the real thing, making at the same time the entirely justified assumption that her private life was as much a matter of public knowledge as that of Madame Bovary: 'Vadim revealed me to myself, Trintignant seduced me, Rojo [a Spanish actor she had met while appearing in *Les Bijoutiers*] fired my passion. Sacha gave me tenderness with every word, with every kiss. But Jacques stole my heart. There will be no more after this.'

The language is indistinguishable from that on the posters that publicized her movies and this was appropriate because it was by now all part of the same story. Bardot was a myth, an icon. The initials themselves had been almost copyrighted, and even those two letters had their own vivacious lewdness – BB, pronounced bébé – resembling in their double curves a providential mimetic tribute to the breasts and buttocks of their possessor, and yet reassuringly and paradoxically meaning 'baby'. The life was part of common currency and increasingly the films themselves became a comment on the life, a spotlight on the phenomenon. But if the art has become the life and the life is itself the art, what space is left for the private emotions?

BB, an icon . . .

...and an object of adoration

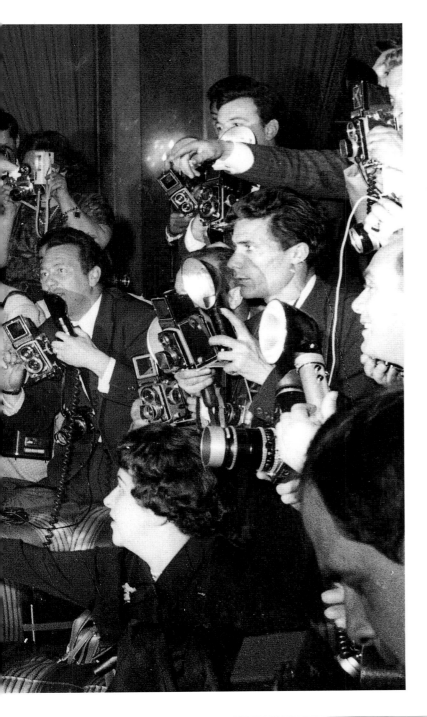

This was the world that Jacques Charrier was marrying into. The *Observer* commented from its vantage point on the other side of the Channel that Bardot's second husband 'M. Jacques Charrier, the actor, has a solid reliable look about him.' From closer up this would prove not to be the case. He was a talented, strikingly handsome but unstable young man, quite unfit to bear the attention he was about to receive. The pressure increased with news of Bardot's pregnancy. She had always insisted to Vadim that she had no interest in motherhood and he, flattering or comforting himself perhaps, believed that she only became pregnant because he had recently become a father with his new partner, Annette Stroyberg. Whatever the reason, the prospect of Bardot becoming a mother increased the attention devoted to her.

In the post-war years, while female stars were demonstrating their essential ordinariness by becoming pregnant, their male counterparts made the same gesture by entering the army for national service. Just a couple of years earlier, Elvis Presley had revealed he was a decent American boy by permitting the notorious hair to be cut short, after which he was transported to a base in Germany for a year to serve his country. Not so well remembered was the attempt to emulate Presley's example by the 'English Elvis', Terry Dene, who was called up for his military service amid carefully instigated publicity but was then quickly discharged because of flat feet. Bardot's relationship with Jean-Louis Trintignant had been disrupted by his military service and now Charrier, in his turn, was called up, shortly after their marriage. The imperious star, however, was not to be denied the presence of her consort and she arranged compassionate leave for him so that they would not be separated during

A pigtailed Bardot with an arm around her 'solid,
reliable-looking' second husband, Jacques Charrier,
in 1959

*The pert young starlet,
beautifully caught in the early
fifties by Philippe Halsman*

RIGHT

Bardot demonstrating the innocent sexuality that she personified in the years before God re-created her as a pouting blonde

OPPOSITE

The icon: in the late fifties Bardot was the most famous actress in the world

LEFT

The erotic image, often on the verge — sometimes over the edge — of tackiness

ABOVE

Brigitte Bardot and Michel Piccoli, with references to Fritz Lang and Dean Martin in Jean-Luc Godard's masterpiece, LE MÉPRIS *(1963)*

LEFT

VIVA MARIA! gave Bardot and Jeanne Moreau a rare, if not altogether happy, opportunity to display their genuine comic talent

BELOW

Bardot quietly celebrates her fortieth birthday with a few friends, a pair of boots and a bicycle

Brigitte Bardot growing old with dignity and a dog. It was her other close companion who would prove to be a problem

the pregnancy, a use of privilege that provoked questions in the French parliament. Charrier was compelled to return to barracks, where he was an object alternately of envy and ridicule. He suffered a mental breakdown and was discharged from the army.

After the birth of their son, Nicolas, in 1960, Charrier collapsed once more under the pressure of his new role. Like other companions of Bardot, he found it impossible to cope with the sheer immensity of what she represented, a beautiful, successful woman, who was at the same time almost a national resource, and now a mother as well. As he once put it: 'You can't have for yourself what belongs to the whole of the country, whether it is Brigitte Bardot or Camembert cheese.'

LEFT

After the birth of Nicolas in 1960: Bardot seems on her way to somewhere else and the strain is starting to show on her husband

If marriage and motherhood had been a tactic to win her the love of the French people then it was a failure, since she was either unable or unwilling to see it through. The unfortunate Charrier was abandoned and she caused public outrage by announcing her dislike of motherhood with no attempt at tactful hypocrisy: 'I am no mother and I won't be one.' Nicolas was returned to the care of his father and his father's family and she would scarcely see him again until his late teenage years. Brigitte/Juliette/Yvette had been talked of as a woman for whom everything was just appetite. If she saw a man she desired she would just help herself to him. In much the same spirit she had tried a baby, hadn't much cared for it and had given it back, or as Marguerite Duras would put it, with that instinctive empathy that people traditionally assume when writing about Bardot, 'because she did not have the means to behave like a real mother to the child who would have become a rival of herself.'

Bardot had made some trivial films since *En cas de malheur*, but now she agreed to work with one of the greatest of French directors, Henri-Georges Clouzot, who was also well-known in Britain and America due to the international success of his brilliantly grim 1955 thriller, *The Wages of Fear*, about French exiles in South America compelled by poverty to undertake the almost suicidal task of delivering two lorry-loads of nitro-glyc-erine across some impossibly rugged territory (it is to be used to extinguish the fire raging on an oil field). Clouzot was known for his intensely pessimistic vision, and for the demands he made on actors for the ruthless-ness with which he realized it in his films.

Together they made *La Vérité* (*The Truth*) a court-room drama about a young woman (played by Bardot) who is on trial for the murder of her sister's fiancé (played by the handsome young actor, Sami Frey). As the witnesses give evidence, Dominique's story is told in a series of flashbacks. That Dominique has killed the young man is not in doubt, the question is whether it was a pre-meditated crime or a spontaneous act against an ex-lover who had brutally spurned her. The court is informed in great detail about Dominique's life, circumstances and attitudes. She had left the respectable family home to share a flat with her well-behaved sister, a dutiful daugh-ter and student at a Paris music college. Dominique is self-indulgent and wilful, whether in neglecting domestic details or entering into casual sexual relationships in the bohemian milieu which she soon inhabits. She begins an affair, and falls in love, with her sister's boyfriend but loses him because of her own unthinking behaviour.

Bardot contemplated by her new lover, Sami Frey, in Clouzot's LA VÉRITÉ

What is on trial is not just a single crime but a way of life which is incomprehensible to the bourgeois folk on the jury and the bench. Sexual fidelity is simply not important to Dominique and when she slips into a form of prostitution to raise money, even that is not the devastating fall that it might seem. A clash between generations is masquerading as an objective legal process. The witnesses are young bohemians – compelled to articulate the codes of a lifestyle that they take for granted – or baffled, disapproving older people. Clouzot shrewdly anticipates the trials that were going to take place in Europe and the United States in which new styles of behaviour as much as specific points of law were at issue (exchanges in *La Vérité* strikingly resemble disputes that were about to take place between judges and witnesses in such British cases as the Lady Chatterley Trial in 1960 and the trial of Mick Jagger and Keith Richard on minor drug possession charges in 1967).

Yet there is something banal about a single person standing for a generation or, for that matter, about giving much importance to the ideas of generations at all, and Clouzot probes deeper than that. The audience catches on early in the film to the mild social criticism in the observation that it is Dominique's (and Brigitte Bardot's) way of life that is on trial. The tragic conclusion is that Dominique's individualistic behaviour leads to her being rejected even by the generation that she has been portrayed as symbolizing. Clouzot had seen from Bardot's own experience, either as represented in the press or presented on film in *And God Created Woman*, that her personal sexual revolution was being conducted in a vacuum, that her own supposedly novel morality was not matched by any significant shift among contemporary

men. They might be happy to conduct a brief affair with her but when it came to settling down in marriage they sought a respectable Mrs Distel. This distinction – between the women one slept with and the woman one married – was a perfectly traditional one and if a woman one slept with happened to believe that she was doing something different, well, that was irrelevant.

The painful conclusion of *La Vérité* is that in order to be found innocent, Dominique will have to destroy her own fragile sense of self by admitting publicly that the one man she loved actually cared nothing for her and that it was in response to that sudden realization that she killed him. The conflict is insupportable for her and the night before the verdict is to be announced she commits suicide by slashing her wrists. The trial is wound up, the lawyers move on to another case.

'He knew how to drag emotions from me that I had never even suspected': Clouzot and Bardot on the set of LA VÉRITÉ

Many people consider this to be Bardot's finest film and it won some major prizes, including the Academy Award for the Best Foreign Film. There have also been detractors, most prominently Pauline Kael, who denounced it as a 'tired and trite and mechanical piece of slick moviemaking'. She argued that the title and structure of the film seemed designed to be in the tradition of *Citizen Kane* or *Rashomon*, in which the different witnesses, each with their own perspective, show us the relativity of truth. One answer to this objection might be that Clouzot shows that it was unnecessary to quibble about events when there was such profound disagreement between and within generations about the meaning of Dominique/Bardot. The irony of the film's title is that the trial was not aimed at establishing the objective truth but merely about expressing different views of society, in particular about establishing the repressive, normative view exemplified by the nun seen in the opening shot of the film who is Dominique's gaoler. If the actual events had been in question as well, then the film would have been chaotic.

Crucially, the film was about Bardot and it was precisely this that Kael objected to. She compared it to what she saw as Marilyn Monroe's similarly meretricious role in John Huston's 1961 film, *The Misfits*, written for Monroe by her husband, Arthur Miller: 'In the pre-Freudian age, the exploitation of personal ailments in films like *The Misfits* and *La Vérité* would have been regarded as disgusting. It is disgusting, and the condescending type of sympathetic "understanding" which is now widely purveyed is an insult to Freud and man. In the frivolous, absurd old days, stars were photographed in their bubble baths: now they bathe in tears of self-pity – while intellectual critics tap their understanding typewriters.'

OPPOSITE

Bardot, Frey and friend stroll on a Paris street

These films were influenced by Freud (and Freud himself would doubtless have insisted that it was no coincidence that John Huston's next film was *Freud*, a biography of the founder of psychoanalysis, for which the original script had been written by Simone de Beauvoir's companion, Jean-Paul Sartre). Crudely speaking, Freud had advocated the breaking down of the barriers we build between our waking and our dream worlds, and this in its turn challenged artists of all kinds to break down the distinction between their lives and their work. While poets like Robert Lowell and Sylvia Plath were transcribing their breakdowns in their poetry, eliminating old notions of privacy, it seemed natural for film directors to do the same. A crucial tenet of the French cinema at the beginning of the sixties was that film should be about the experience of watching film and making film. When asked why there was so much blood in *Pierrot le fou* Jean-Luc Godard replied that it wasn't blood but red. In the same spirit, the major film directors who worked with Bardot realized, or decided, that there was no point in having Bardot pretend to be an ordinary girl because there was no longer any honourable way of creating the suspension of disbelief and therefore you had to use Bardot to explore the idea of Bardot herself, or itself.

This led to further problems, among them the effect on the people concerned in human terms. The suicides of poets like John Berryman, Sylvia Plath and Anne Sexton suggest that there are dangers in using yourself as your own tragic subject. The experience of making *La Vérité* was extremely demanding for Bardot. A legend grew up surrounding the film, stories that Clouzot had tormented and even struck Bardot in order to goad her into producing the performance he wanted. Looking back, thirty years later, Bardot described it unequivocally as the only film in which she was a real actress, and indeed, though she is only playing a version of herself which she had played before, she does it far more unsparingly here, with moments of truly lacerating self-exposure. She has to put herself on screen, as she had before, but now she had to be humiliated and rejected. She denied that Clouzot had ever hit her but conceded that he had deliberately undermined her in many different ways: 'He knew how to provoke tears from me and

drag emotions from me that I had never even suspected.'

The most immediately deleterious effects of the filming were not on Bardot but on Jacques Charrier, and these were provoked not by Clouzot's uncompromising behaviour but by Bardot's affair with her co-star, Sami Frey, and by Charrier's sense of humiliation at the sex scenes that his estranged wife was performing. Wholesomely or not, Vadim had been able to use, and perhaps transcend, this humiliation by capturing it on film. No such release was available to Charrier, who assaulted Frey and twice attempted suicide during the shooting. For her own part, Bardot finished the film 'at the end of my tether, physically, emotionally and psychologically.' Looking back, she said that she had forgotten all the difficult aspects of the role and that she regretted nothing. At the time it may have seemed different.

Bardot's films were related to her life in a complicated way, influenced by her life and then going on to influence it. *And God Created Woman* was, to some extent, based on her own character, and it seems clear that she herself felt compelled (or perhaps liberated) to follow the example of the character she played in pursuing her own impulses. The court case in *La Vérité* compels Dominique to interrogate herself. A person inventing herself as she goes along is suddenly compelled to explore what she really is. For the first time Bardot may have sensed that her public image had robbed her of a private life. Far from portraying her enviable freedom, it constrained her in a role no less constricting than the repressions of bourgeois respectability that she had supposedly escaped. It may be that Bardot felt that the film had exposed the failure of her life to her or she may have felt that it had told her story and that she was trapped by

the course of its narrative as if by fate. She may also have started to worry about her age. In *And God Created Woman* she was twenty-two playing seventeen, in *La Vérité* she was twenty-five playing twenty-two.

Shortly after shooting had been completed, she celebrated her twenty-fifth birthday, having dinner with Clouzot. Later that evening she took an overdose of barbiturates and cut her wrists in a determined bid to kill herself that almost succeeded. The suicide attempt was generally explained as a natural result of the pressures of her public life and in particular of Clouzot's working methods. Vadim, who briefly returned to her side to help her recover, saw it as nothing to do with her career, her lovers or the details of her life but 'world-weariness'. Whatever the cause, it only served to increase her unpopularity in this still predominantly Catholic country. Bardot had already demonstrated her contempt

for the pieties of family obligation, now she had shown contempt for life itself. In one incident that was always to haunt her, a woman, encountered by chance in a hospital lift, attempted to stab her face with a fork, the first weapon that came to hand, resentful that Bardot had been so heedless of her life when the woman's son, a soldier, had died fighting for France. All the responses to her suicide attempt only echoed the provocations that had driven her to it in the first place, the sense that her privacy was irretrievably lost, dissipated among the public. The chemist who sold Bardot the barbiturates was later asked why he had not recognized and questioned her: 'I serve a hundred Bardots every day,' he replied.

It can be tempting to describe Bardot as a survivor,

particularly in comparison with Marilyn Monroe, who died in 1962 and became a versatile symbol – of the self-destructive film star, the female victim, and much else. In fact it is purely a matter of chance that Bardot survived and Monroe didn't. It could easily have been the other way around: Marilyn Monroe sixty-eight years old, long retired after the decline of her career in the sixties, helpless in the face of changing times and mores. According to some people who knew her, though Bardot survived and recovered from her suicide attempt, something was permanently lost. She would never again let herself be as vulnerable as she had been.

Her choice of films remained as wayward as ever. She was re-united with Vadim once more to star in *Le Repos du guerrier* (*Warrior's Rest*: the British film censors refused to allow it under its original title, *Love on a Pillow*, which was con-

OPPOSITE _____

Back with Vadim for LE REPOS DU GUERRIER, *1962*

sidered too sexually explicit). Lightning failed to strike twice. The film was so bad that an Italian movie critic asked rhetorically why 'a country like France seriously accepts Vadim, who has the culture of a platypus, the taste of a Jayne Mansfield and no talent. The film contains enough boredom to last an entire generation.'

Yet at the same time Bardot was filming with one of the finest young directors working in French cinema, Louis Malle. The original plan, bizarre as it may seem, was to produce a French adaptation of Noël Coward's play, *Private Lives*. This idea was quickly dropped but since the project had already been announced, it was decided to stick, more or less, with the original title and the film was called *Vie privée* (*A Very Private Affair*). Once again the concept of Bardot herself became the main subject, as Malle recalled years later: 'I thought it might be interesting to try to recreate in the film the strange social phenomenon that Brigitte Bardot had become, the sex object who had become an object of scandal. In her way she was a pioneer of the feminist movement. She was not political, but she had decided to live her life as a man might; to be the equal of men on every level.'

Vie privée, though, is not about feminism but about the price of Bardot's celebrity. Before writing the script, Malle and Jean-Paul Rappeneau talked a great deal to her and incorporated details from her life into the story. The film begins with an idyllic, bohemian pre-fame Bardot, all the more poignant because it is as if Bardot is mourning not a life that she has lost but one that she never had and will now never be able to attain. She quickly and improbably (though little less improbably than Bardot herself) becomes a film star – there is an amusing parody of a Vadim-style sex scene, which we see being dubbed by Bardot while functionaries of the studio stare at her through the glass. The manipulation of her image by producers and the pursuit of her by photographers and the press make her life unbearable.

One interesting aspect of Bardot's fame shown by Malle, already as early as 1962, is the influence she was starting to have. An eerie sequence shot in a Paris street leads the audience to think they are looking at Bardot until they see in each case that it is another woman who has imitated her appearance. Bardot's character begins an affair with a journalist and theatre director (played by Marcello Mastroianni) and she flees the pressures of France to hide out with him in Spoleto in Italy, where he is directing a play. She attracts the attention first of the locals, then of the international press until her presence

LEFT

Preparing to shoot a scene with Marcello Mastroianni in VIE PRIVÉE (1961)

OVERLEAF

Bardot imitating Bardot, a crowd pretending to be a crowd, in VIE PRIVÉE

begins to make rehearsals of the open-air production impossible and she becomes a virtual prisoner in her rented apartment.

Vie privée is a modish, rather slick film, making use of the then fashionable technique of the freeze frame to punctuate the action. (It had been famously used by François Truffaut at the climax of his feature film debut, *Les Quatres Cents Coups*.) The entire enterprise has its ludicrous side, a feature film starring a sex goddess virtually playing herself lamenting about not being left alone to live a quiet life. Hollywood had dealt with this subject rather more intelligently and less self-pityingly for many years, whether comically in, for example, *Singin' in the Rain* (in which the silent star and dumb blonde, Lena Lamont, assures her fans at a movie première that 'if we have brought a little happiness into your drab lives then all our hard work and suffering ain't been in vain for nothing') or seriously, in George Cukor's version of *A Star is Born* in which Judy Garland, in caring for James Mason, and as it were being displaced from the destruction of her own life by the pressures of stardom, is able to contemplate her situation all the more poignantly. Unlike Clouzot (who is all too clear about the almost intolerable, chaotic irresponsibility of Dominique in *La Vérité*, as well as her desperate vulnerability), Malle indulges Bardot, not interrogating sufficiently her need for attention which alternates with the desire for obscurity. But Malle has a fine eye for moments which illuminate Bardot's life, the yearning glances she gives at people who can wander anonymously in the street or, even more powerfully, when she looks at the paparazzi

OPPOSITE

A relatively quiet moment between actress and director, Louis Malle

camped outside her mother's house, and suddenly realizes that even they have a sense of community among themselves that is denied to her, their prey.

Beauvoir's essay, 'Brigitte Bardot and the Lolita Syndrome', had been written for the American magazine *Esquire*, and not translated into French at the time (reflecting, perhaps, certain qualms on Beauvoir's part – she is very harsh about French attitudes towards women – and also a less than pressing desire on the behalf of French people to read an analysis of their country's most famous living icon). Louis Malle read it during shooting and translated for Bardot who had not seen it: 'She laughed and laughed, and said, "It's nothing to do with me!" But actually it was pretty accurate in describing what Bardot represented at the time – this object of scandal and controversy.'

Vie privée works best in the largely improvised sequences down in the more relaxed setting of Spoleto. Bardot and Mastroianni notoriously took against each other, which Malle speaks of with regret, but in fact this palpable air of disenchantment tellingly reinforces our sense of Bardot's isolation. The film ends in flamboyantly over-the-top style when Bardot, clambering over a roof to view the play's first night from which she has been excluded by her bitter lover, is blinded by a photographer's flash and falls to her death in operatic style like Tosca or Senta. Unsurprisingly, perhaps, this letter of complaint despatched by Louis Malle and Brigitte Bardot was a resounding commercial and critical failure. The public would remain obsessed with Bardot herself but henceforth would be more willing to leave her films in peace.

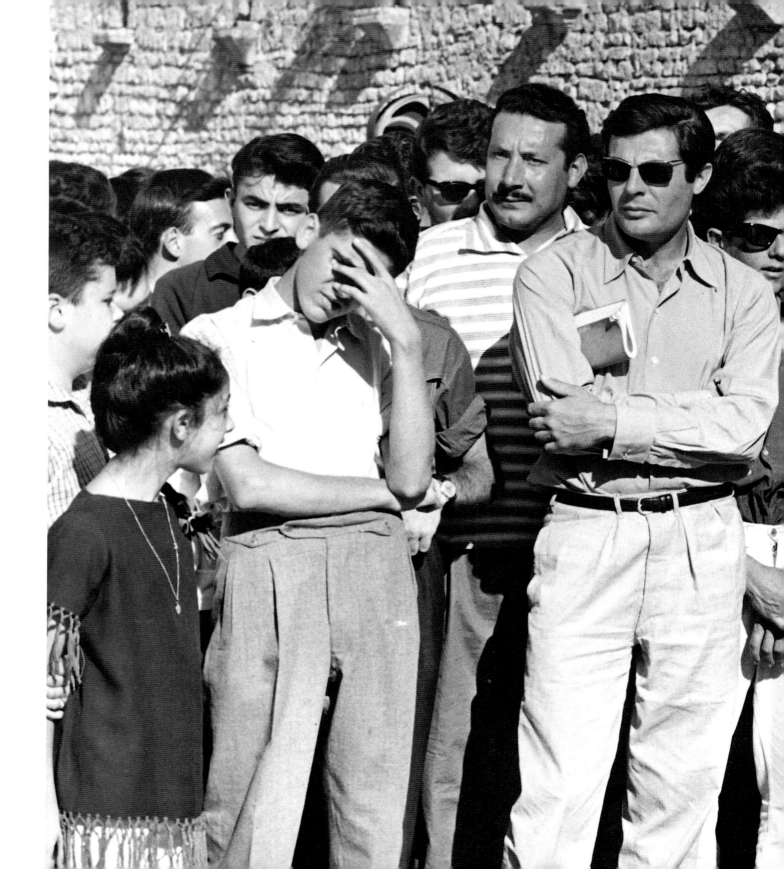

Relations between Bardot and Mastroianni during shooting were chilly

OPPOSITE

*Preparing for the operatic
climax of* VIE PRIVÉE

LEFT

*Bardot — 'this object of
scandal and controversy' —
goes shopping*

Je me donne
à qui me plaît

rigitte Bardot's career as a singer is scarcely even known of outside France. French pop music is one of those strange, domestic products — like haggis from Scotland, fermented fish from Scandinavia, warm beer from Britain — that is unexportable because nobody else shows any sign of liking it. To non-French ears, it sounds like an unsatisfactory hybrid of watered-down rock and roll with jollied-up Jacques Brel. And just as French actors like Jean-Paul Belmondo and Gérard Départieu make comedies and cop films that nobody outside France sees, French actresses like Isabelle Adjani, Jeanne Moreau and Catherine Deneuve make records that nobody outside France hears.

In the context of this genre, Bardot is a talented performer and in fact the affection that she finally, gradually, wrung out of the French public derived far more from her musical work than from her films — her New Year's Eve singing-and-dancing spectacular was a particular favourite and became a tradition on French television. In her films of the early sixties she had painfully opened herself up to scrutiny, showing a darker side of the sun-drenched Mediterranean nymph and the commercial results had been disappointing. Her songs also put her on display, but in a determinedly light-hearted way, by travestying her image, providing a coarse, impermeable lowest-common-denominator version of the BB legend for tourists, the sort of people who would drive down to

ABOVE

The unknown Bardot — balladeer

OPPOSITE

A French television special: the wholesome family entertainer in leather boots

Saint-Tropez and ruin the ambience by dropping litter and setting up hot dog stands.

The songs are personal statements written by other people on her behalf and their vision of Bardot seems to derive from accounts of her life in the popular press, set to a Eurovision beat. Among her 1962 releases are songs with titles like 'Je me donne à qui me plaît' and 'Invitango', the latter of which begins:

Je vous invite à l'indécenc'
De ce tango presque argentin
Où je ferai la connaissanc'
De votre corps contre le mien

(I invite you to the indecency of this tango, almost Argentine, where I will get to know your body against mine.)

The subject matter or style did not alter substantially over the years. Bardot's neo-Cartesian hymn to the discothèque (a word, incidentally, that Roger Vadim has claimed the dubious honour for inventing, back in his days in Saint-Germain des Prés), 'Je dance donc je suis' dates from 1964. Six years later, at a time when her popularity as a film star was fading fast, she recorded songs like 'Nue au soleil',

Quand le printemps
Fait éclater tous les bourgeons
Mes vêtements
Me pèsent d'une étrange façon

(When the spring makes the buds open in passion, my clothes start to weigh down on me in a strange fashion.)

and, 'Tu veux ou tu veux pas', a cheery hymn to Bardot's fabled sexual nonchalance:

Tu veux ou tu veux pas
Tu veux c'est bien, si tu veux pas tant pis

(You want to or you don't want to, if you do want to, that's fine, if you don't want to, too bad.)

These songs sit a little curiously with the actress who had appeared in tormented films like *La Vérité* and *Vie Privée*, who had made a serious attempt at suicide, who had complained of being harried by her fans. It is almost as if Greta Garbo in her retirement had moonlighted as a go-go dancer. Yet it seems to have been a conscious strategy. On the evidence of the films she was to make, the music is symptomatic of a deliberate change to her public image, a conscious coarsening. Never again would she open herself up in the way that she had been encouraged to do as early as *And God Created Woman*, let alone explore her anxieties on screen with the intimacy that had been prompted by Clouzot and Malle.

The quintessential Bardot in 1962: ruffled hair, rumpled sheets, smoking cigarette

The process may have been aided by the process of her own look catching up with her. Bardot had been at her most beautiful in *La Vérité* and *Vie Privée*. She seemed to have benefited from her years of success spent in the sun, eating, drinking, dancing, making love, sleeping, if we can believe the evidence of her songs. She now had the money and the time to make her hair look truly natural and it had attained a new opulence, like the mane of a bleached lion. Its texture was unique, light and airy, always appearing as if it had just been spread out between the rumpled sheets of somebody else's bed. In the late fifties, as American films became bolder and actresses began to be glimpsed in realistic bedroom settings, the incongruity between the rumpled sheets and their immaculate hairstyles and full make-up was frequently comical but in those two films Bardot had looked at her best when disturbed in bed, sinfully late on a weekday morning, her locks in the most beautifully

Bardot's influence was pervasive, whether on successive partners of Roger Vadim, Catherine Deneuve and Jane Fonda, or major new stars like Julie Christie

arranged disarray. But her uniqueness could only be temporary. Malle had shown in *Vie privée* how other girls were imitating the Bardot look. Now there was a new generation of actresses whose look derived from Bardot and were rivals, if only because they were younger and Bardot's image was based on youthfulness, both physically and psychologically, the supple skin and the impudent attitude. Two of them – Catherine Deneuve and Jane Fonda – were successive partners of Roger Vadim and with others like Julie Christie, they would be embodiments of the sixties in a way which Bardot, to whom they owed so much, could never be. A 1993 British newspaper profile described Bardot as the 'embodiment of tack' a phrase that would have been unthinkable in the fifties. If you represent impulsiveness, what happens when a generation imitates you? If you embody youth, what happens when you grow old?

At this moment of change in 1963, Bardot made what is arguably her finest film, and certainly one of her most controversial, *Le Mépris* (known in Britain and America as *Contempt*), directed by Jean-Luc Godard. It was a time, that now seems inconceivable, when American producers, aware of the bankruptcy of ideas in Hollywood cinema, saw opportunities in the vibrant, young films being produced in Europe. With bizarre naivety, Joseph Levine hired Jean-Luc Godard to make a big-budget adaptation of Alberto Moravia's novel, *A Ghost at Noon*, with Bardot hired – for a reputed fee of half a million dollars – as an added attraction. Godard was even contractually obliged to shoot some nude scenes. What could go wrong?

To those who knew Godard's earlier work (and it appears that Levine had not actually taken the trouble to see a Godard film), it was no surprise that he produced a work that was really about the idea of a crass American producer hiring Europeans to make a film about the *Odyssey. Le Mépris* has an outstanding cast. Jack Palance gives a flamboyantly corrosive performance as the predatory producer, for whom art, power and money are indistinguishable: 'When I hear the word culture, I reach for my chequebook,' he says. Michel Piccoli is the ruefully self-loathing playwright hired to doctor the script. Bardot plays his beautiful wife: his muse, siren and tormentor. The director of the film-within-the-film is the great Fritz Lang, then at the end of one of the greatest directorial careers in film history, playing himself. Unlike Godard's later, more crudely didactic work, *Le Mépris* is a complicated, torn film. Raoul Coutard, the film's cinematographer, described it as Godard's 'letter to his wife', the actress, Anna Karina – like so many others, from Beauvoir to Malle, Godard was able to use Bardot as a symbol. His hero, Piccoli, despises himself for accepting dollars from a man he despises, yet he adores the American cinema (he wears a little pork-pie hat throughout, 'comme Dean Martin en *Some Came Running*'). Godard saw Bardot as the quintessential object of desire and he had no interest in her psychology or the details of her private life, which suited Bardot herself as well. This is by far the best film about the public Bardot and the idea of woman as a passive emblem. If Bardot is Piccoli's inspiration, she is also his excuse. He claims that it is only for her that he is corrupting himself by accepting the money, yet at the same time he tormentedly, aggressively steers her into Palance's arms and ultimately into running away with Palance (which results in her almost comically melodramatic death in a car

LEFT _____

Bardot, Jean-Luc Godard and the wig he put her in for LE MÉPRIS (1963)

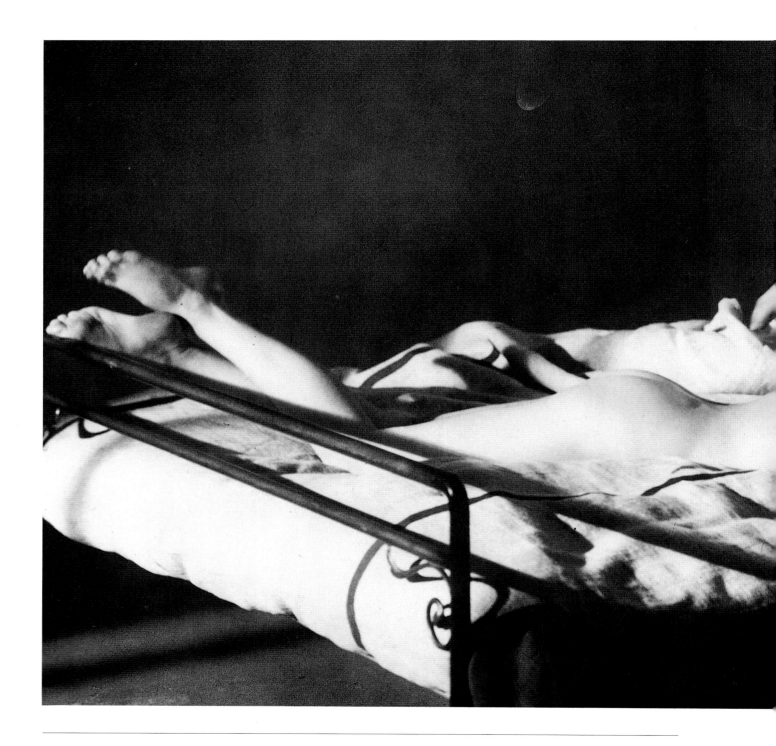

crash). Once again, a great director has interrogated the mixture of love and fear that Roger Vadim had only toyed with in *And God Created Woman*.

Godard at this period was obsessed with the idea of cinema and *Le Mépris'* constant subject is film itself and it is obsessively self-reflexive. Fritz Lang denounces the widescreen Cinemascope format in which, needless to say, *Le Mépris* is shot, as fit only for snakes and funerals. Yet the affirmation at the end, after all the betrayal and corruption, is that Lang insists on completing the film-within-the-film, the ultimate example of artistic integrity, even in a depraved industry. Godard's consciousness of film also made him extremely sensitive to Bardot's earlier work, and much of her role is a comment on the absurdity of so much in her earlier films. The tone is set in the opening scene in which Bardot lies naked, face down on a bed, in conversation with Piccoli, asking him whether he likes her feet, her thighs, her back, her breasts and so on – her body, this machine of desire, broken down into its component parts and examined.

LEFT

The opening scene of LE MÉPRIS, *inserted at the insistence of the producers*

Godard is both cooperating with the letter of Levine's demands and critically subverting them. We constantly see Bardot as we have seen her in other films, lying in the bath, walking around wrapped in a towel, sunbathing and swimming in the nude. Yet in each case we are disoriented by Godard's detached technique of long takes and unusual camera angles. (There was particular dismay among the film's producers about a sequence of dialogue between Bardot and Piccoli in their apartment that lasts over twenty minutes. Yet, as Godard might have answered, it contains all the incidental thrills

RIGHT

The American producer of *LE MÉPRIS* wanted a bathroom scene, but not this kind

that earlier Bardot films contained, and for which she was hired, her getting in and out of the bath, for example – though while she is in the bath she is reading a critical study of Fritz Lang, which was not the sort of thing we saw in *Une Parisienne*.)

Le Mépris was greeted with dismay, both by the film's producers, who disowned it, and by many critics. Stanley Kauffmann, the distinguished film critic of the decidedly upmarket American magazine, *New Republic*, dismissed the film as of no value, except for those 'interested in Brigitte Bardot's behind'. Yet as both Vadim and Godard knew, this very much *was* part of the point. The reception of *And God Created Woman* established that worldwide interest in Bardot's naked body was an irrefutable fact. Vadim stripped away the cinematic mystery with which screen sex had previously been clothed. Godard interrogates Bardot's naked body as an object on which we project our notions of desire and jealousy, virtue and immorality.

Kauffmann was particularly infuriated by the long apartment scene which, he contended, 'could serve in all film schools as an archetype of arrant egotism and bankrupt imagination in a director.' Yet today the film looks not just like an unequivocal masterpiece, but terribly funny, sprightly, fired with an energetic sense of cinema's possibilities. Truffaut said that every film should be about the joy of moviemaking and *Le Mépris*, despite its veneer of cynicism, now seems almost boyishly idealistic in its commitment to the film form. As Godard himself put it, the film 'proves in 149 shots that in the cinema as in life there is no secret, nothing to elucidate, merely the need to live – and to make films.' Bardot herself, an actress frequently criticised for her limitations and her caution,

deserves credit for her whole-hearted support of a project that was clearly, even wildly, uncommercial, shot in long, highly demanding takes. If she allowed herself to be used as a blank slate on which Godard could write, then that itself is an undervalued ability which she shares with some of the greatest of screen actors, from Gary Cooper to Greta Garbo. When Jane Fonda, a busier, more assertive actress worked with Godard in *Tout va bien* in 1972 (admittedly at a low point in his career when he was hamstrung by his ideological loyalties), the result was hectoring and dull.

In 1963 Bardot met and began a long affair with Bob Zaguri, a South American businessman. Much of it was spent in Brazil and in the milieu to which he introduced her, an existence of parties, pools, après ski and jet travel with people in gold chains, open-necked shirts, honey suntans and lots of money. The change was probably inevitable now that she was approaching thirty. She had already invented a liberating, subversive style for being young, but that had been intuitive. Might she now be able to do the same for growing old? At her thirtieth birthday party she gave a beautifully poised speech which suggested that it might be so: 'The ideal age is the age I am now. At this age one is old enough to know what one is doing and young enough to do it all the same. I am thirty but there are things about me that are still fifteen. I have gone through much in my life and yet I do not feel that I have suffered great tragedies. I love to love and I hate to leave, but I love freely and I leave freely.'

Everything she said was a poignant reminder of how much being young is different from growing older, and how the same action done by a girl of seventeen and a woman of thirty has a different meaning. Beauvoir had

In 1963 Bardot entered the jet set with new boyfriend, Bob Zaguri, and a politically incorrect coat

Bardot at thirty, looking less
young gracefully

asserted that among Bardot's distinctive qualities was her ability to remain untouched by experience. This was liberating because women were traditionally not free from their past in the way that men were, and they were defined, specifically by their sexual – or lack of sexual – experience. Events bounce off the young Bardot and the characters she played leaving them untouched (unless, that is, they are destroyed by external forces, by the rigours of the law in *La Vérité* or by male jealousy in *En cas de malheur*). Yet the Bardot celebrated by Beauvoir (who was then in her early fifties) was partly an idealized figure created by a woman who knew that women, like men, are always affected by life in the end. Juliette in *And God Created Woman* can enticingly pretend to be free of restraints but by the time a man or woman has become thirty, he or she has been visibly defined by experience.

Bardot's thirtieth birthday was the occasion for a reflection by another of France's leading women of letters, Marguerite Duras. This was a grimmer, less adulatory view than that of Beauvoir, five years earlier. She detected a hardening: 'A slight puckering of the mouth and eyes, which yesterday was not there. Yesterday, facing the world, this face was majestically carefree. Today she keeps a close watch on it. That is the difference – her pose. In other words, fear. Is this the end of a dazzling morning? Of course not – but already the warning songs of evening are here. An evening full of wolves.'

Bardot's very opacity as a character, her inability to shift her identity from role to role, turned her into a symbol that both film directors and writers were eager to explore. The directors spoke on her behalf and the writers wrote of her with a sense of uncanny empathy, as if Bardot were a character they had invented and to whose motives they had privileged access. Duras, who was not a friend of Bardot's, told her readers that the actress, though generally seen in public, was essentially a lonely person and intensely bored in her private life. She moved between her various houses, decorated by other people, inventing methods to kill time. Duras insisted that though this sounded harsh it was with the candour of true sympathy: 'It is not out of spite that I speak like this of our idol. People often talk about her but rarely seriously. She deserves that now and then somebody should talk of her power and mystery without lying.' Bardot had always said that when she loved, she loved completely, and Duras agreed that Bardot was completely devoted to her lovers while she lived with them, but this intense devotion to the moment of love was itself an attempt to freeze time artificially: 'I am certain that she has never known the end of a love affair, the heartbreaking depression of loneliness and liberty. But she knows that other tragedy of starting afresh right away. Has she ever paused between two romances – got her second wind – has she ever done this? I don't think so.'

At the time she wrote her essay on Bardot, Beauvoir's own liaison with a younger man, Claude Lanzmann (who would later make *Shoah*, the celebrated documentary about the Holocaust), was just breaking up. A biographer of Beauvoir has argued that behind her essay was the need to create a woman who would not be damaged by being left, who would not suffer the particular pain of a woman growing old, that she felt

OPPOSITE _____

Hampstead, North London, in 1963, blending in with the natives. Bardot's the one in the boots

inescapable in her own life. The memorable conclusion to the essay – 'I hope she will mature, but not change' – was as much about her own impending old age. In a similar way, it could be argued that Duras was asking Bardot to become a Duras character, or even to become Marguerite Duras herself, to savour the failure of love and our vulnerability to it and to time, rather than to believe herself untouched. Like Beauvoir, Duras noted Bardot's impermeability: 'Although she has left many corpses in her wake, she herself remains unharmed. This is what I mean when I say that nothing has ever happened to her yet.'

Beauvoir had set Bardot on a pedestal to fight a battle on behalf of other women and of Beauvoir herself.

The pendulum had now swung the other way and Duras saw that this notion of youthful resilience was itself a trap. Bardot's youthful insouciance, freed from traditional moral constraints, was subversive in its own way but not only was it an ideal that other women would inevitably fail to live up to, it would also defeat Bardot herself year by year. Beauvoir vaingloriously called on Bardot to ignore the passing of time; five years later Duras hoped that she would yield to it: 'I am sorry that nothing more important has happened to Bardot than to be our idol; that a very strong wind never encountered before has not blown across these last few years; that she has never committed a great and noble mistake. But how can this be averted even if we wished it? One day she will discover that what is happening to her is neither more or less than the fate of all human beings and nothing else.'

Yet there seemed no immediate cause for alarm.

Despite never having gone to Hollywood, Bardot's earning capacity was very healthy indeed, and she was now able to demand an average fee of around £100,000 plus a percentage of the film's gross earnings. For her new film with Louis Malle, *Viva Maria!* in 1965, she was paid a good deal more, around £150,000, almost twice what her co-star, Jeanne Moreau, received.

Malle has always led a career of contrasts, moving between Europe and America, documentaries and features, small and large scale projects. His previous feature film had been the sombre masterpiece, *Le Feu follet*, very French, claustrophobic, shot in grim black and white, about the events leading up to a man's suicide. This he had followed with *Bons baisers de Bangkok*, a fifteen-minute documentary for French television about everyday life in the Thai capital. Now he decided to make a big comedy, a frivolous, picaresque adventure film shot in Mexico. With a slyness characteristic of Malle, the light tone of the film obscures the fact that its subject matter concerns terrorism, violent revolution and some savage, occasionally blasphemous, anti-clericalism.

Bardot plays Maria O'Malley, the daughter of a French mother and an Irish Republican terrorist father and in the superb opening sequences of the film we see her aiding him in the planting of bombs in Britain and around the Empire. In 1907 he is killed as they blow up a bridge in an anonymous Central American country and Maria escapes into the jungle. She stumbles across a travelling circus, witnesses the suicide of a young woman and takes her place in a double act with another woman, also called Maria (Jeanne Moreau). The pair are an immense success with their charmingly innocent striptease act and they also get involved with the armed insurgence against

the country's brutal military dictatorship, finally becoming active participants and then leaders of the rebellion that, at the end of the film, sweeps the country's tyrant (and the reactionary Catholic Church) from power.

The best parts of the film are the (violently anti-British) early sequences – at the same time lyrical, comic and violent – showing Maria as a girl and then an adolescent aiding her father. After her father's death Maria disguises herself as a boy, hair up under a cap, face carefully dirtied, and there are tantalizing hints of what a good comic performer she could have been. Even Pauline Kael, who considered the pairing of Bardot and Moreau to be a failure, was grudgingly won over by this part of the film: 'But Bardot – not because of any *acting* – has never been more enchanting than in parts of this movie. When Malle put her into boys' clothes, with a cap and a smudge on her cheek, she was a tomboy looking for fun: Zazie grown up but still polymorphously amoral.'

As he later recalled, Malle had cast the film almost out of a mischievous sense of not being able to resist a challenge: 'I was the only one who could put Bardot and Moreau together in a film and make it work. I would never do it again, much as I like them. It transformed the film into something else.' The project suddenly became far larger and, in Malle's own words, 'I was carried away and this pastiche of an adventure film becomes *really* an adventure film, with an enormous number of extras. And it lost a bit of its bite.' The pairing of these two great, but hugely contrasting, stars was a subject of avid curiosity in the French media and the shooting of the film itself became a circus, with reporters eager to find evidence of rivalry between the two actresses. The relations between them were perfectly civilized but Bardot

was not easy to deal with. Famously resistant to working outside France, she arrived two weeks late at Cuernavaca in Mexico, where the film was shot, accompanied by Pierre Cardin, her boyfriend at the time, and a substantial entourage, as if to replicate the social scene that she was leaving behind in Paris. She provoked some sour comment by (as would be more and more her practice) adopting local stray dogs and feeding them in a locality where the resident humans had difficulty in getting enough to eat.

Enjoyable as much of it is, *Viva Maria!* looks today like a film that went out of control. In its baroque style, its parodic tone, its interest in revolutionary politics, the film anticipates the 'spaghetti westerns' that would be made in Italy and Spain over the next few years and be both lucrative and influential. It could have been a great, wild comedy but unfortunately after the brittle elegance which is so promising in the early scenes, it degenerates – as Malle has regretfully acknowledged – into a coarsely comic action film. Malle lost his grip under the pressure of coordinating an unwieldy production with the demands of the two stars and he speaks of it as the only one of his films that he would like to remake – quickly and cheaply, with two unknown young actresses.

During shooting the film had been portrayed as a contest between Moreau and Bardot, with keen debate over which actress would win. After a private screening, Georges Pompidou, then the president of France, came up to Malle and said simply: 'Moreau won.' For his part, Malle thought Bardot emerged with more credit from the film, partly because Moreau never seems at ease with

OPPOSITE _____

Bardot, 'still polymorphously amoral' in VIVA MARIA!

the flamboyance and theatricality of her role. Bardot promoted the film energetically in America and created
something of a stir but the film was a resounding flop,
too harsh to be a cheery comedy, too broad to appeal to
art house audiences, too subtle and strange to be an easy
mainstream hit. In the rest of the world, though, it was
a substantial commercial success.

Over the next few years Bardot would still be interested in working with France's more distinguished directors but her reputation now tended to count against her.
She began to be seen as intractable and suitable only for a
narrow range of roles, either the broad, light-hearted
tone of *Viva Maria!* or the more familiar roles where she
was essentially playing herself or, worse, coarsened versions of Juliette. At a similar age, both Catherine
Deneuve and Jane Fonda, who had started out looking
like Bardot clones, were able to steer their careers into
other directions. Deneuve in particular, a glacial blonde,
might have been thought to be even more restricted in
her potential roles than Bardot, but she was lucky – or
shrewd – enough to find parts that exploited this and
became, as David Thompson put it, 'a fantastic actress,
her beauty a receptacle for any imagination, perhaps the
greatest cool blonde, for ever hinting at intimations of
depravity'. The problem with Bardot's career was a curious parallel with the failing of her private life in which
men met her for brief affairs but – with or without her
encouragement – went elsewhere when they wanted a
more sustained relationship.

Directors used Bardot when they wanted to explore,
or exploit, the intriguing Bardot image. She never found
anybody with the confidence to cajole her into other
kinds of acting, into experimenting with less obvious

Bardot energetically promoted *VIVA MARIA!* in America but to no avail. The director, Louis Malle, looks beleaguered on her right

RIGHT

A rare moment in Bardot's third marriage to Gunther Sachs, catching the couple together in Tahiti, August 1966

OPPOSITE

A typical moment of affectionate intimacy during the Bardot — Sachs marriage

sides to her talent. Deneuve also made mediocre films with Vadim but she then challenged great directors like Polanski, Buñuel and Truffaut into imagining the madness and perversion that might lie behind the perfect façade that Vadim had contented himself with. Bardot's own image was too resilient, too firmly established in everybody's mind: the public's, directors' and her own. She had obtained an identity as strong as film legends like Greta Garbo and Marilyn Monroe. In 1965 there was even an American feature film called *Dear Brigitte*, a moderately amusing comedy about a precocious eight-year-old (in a family presided over by James Stewart) with a crush on Bardot, who makes a brief appearance. This plot would not have been plausible with any other living actress – not Sophia Loren, Audrey Hepburn or anyone but Bardot – but this extraordinary status inhibited her career, certainly if she wished to make films that were a departure from her usual material. During the sixties she repeatedly offered projects to François Truffaut but he always turned her down. The producers of *La Sirène du Mississippi* tried to insist on her for the role of the *femme fatale* who heedlessly torments, and almost murders, the hopelessly lovesick Jean-Paul Belmondo, but Truffaut, wary of a film that would be dominated by a pouting Bardot, insisted on using Catherine Deneuve – an especially mortifying rejection.

It is difficult to assess the extent to which it was just a matter of chance as well. In June 1966 Joseph Losey, the American director resident in Britain, was keen to star Bardot in his film *La Truite*, a story, he told her, about 'Force, Power, Glamour'. He wrote excitedly in a letter to a colleague about her 'fabulous untouched reserves … as an actress and as a person', but the deal fell through and he wasn't able to make the film for another fifteen years, by which time it starred Isabelle Hupert. The film sank without trace.

In 1966, while she was in the course of an affair with her middle-aged Parisian dentist, Bardot met and quickly married the German millionaire playboy, Gunther Sachs who, at thirty-two, was her age. In her two previous marriages she had made at least a token attempt at a pri-

*The rebellious Bardot was also
always Pilou's daughter*

vate relationship in a settled household. This was, at least, the ideal against which she failed, firstly because of Vadim's indifference to a settled bourgeois existence and secondly because, perhaps, of Charrier's instability, her own impatience, the intolerable demands of motherhood and the public scrutiny that her private life then attracted. Her marriage to Sachs was different, a by-product of her life on the international party circuit. The two of them led a hectically public existence, meeting mainly at parties and restaurants, glimpsing each other across dancefloors, while maintaining separate homes.

If the marriage was an experiment, designed as a vehicle to suit the impulsiveness of her nature, then it was an abject failure. In the autumn of 1966, shortly after getting married, she went to England to make *A Coeur joie* (which was translated as *Two Weeks in September*) and in press interviews was already openly disenchanted with her new husband: 'I give myself entirely, but he lives on compromises and is incapable of giving up his past. He tries to take me into a social life that I detest and have always done my best to avoid.' In her adult life, Bardot again and again attempted to recreate the structured tension of her life at the time when she had fallen in love with Roger Vadim. On the one side there was the enticing bohemian, sexual existence, covertly shared with her lover; yet always there was the strict, bourgeois home presided over by Pilou and Toti that she could return to. Each on its own was unsatisfactory — bourgeois domesticity quickly became claustrophobic; the bohemian life lacked a reassuring structure. That balance, which had been unstable enough at the time, proved impossible to recreate. Certainly Pilou's daughter was offended by Sachs's profligacy: 'Our tastes are so different. He loves everything luxurious, loud, and he loves photographers and publicity. When he gives me a present it has to be a grandiose one, while I would prefer a keyring chosen with love.' The effect of this paean to privacy is spoilt only by being delivered to a journalist. The married couple never lived together, as the bride confessed: 'Of course, it would be normal for me to live all the time with Gunther, but I haven't got a key to his house. Anyway it is a strange and unfamiliar place and it frightens me.'

Never in her life was Bardot so open about the details of her private life as when she talked of her instant incompatibility with her new husband. Even when she was permitted into his Paris apartment, she was dismayed by what she found: 'My apartment is my own work. I live surrounded by books and I have read them all. His library is much more beautiful but you can't read the books. I was really shocked when I found that out!'

About the only thing that Bardot didn't say in her interviews while making *A Coeur joie*, was that she was having a brief affair with her co-star, the English minor hearthrob, Mike Sarne (who, apart from that role, is now best forgotten as the director of the legendary fiasco, the screen version of Gore Vidal's *Myra Breckinridge*, in 1970). The affair echoed, in a rather tired way, the story of the film, about the mistress of an older man who has a fling with a younger man and cannot decide between the two. If life was imitating art here, it was because life seemed to have run out of ideas.

If Don Juan Were a Woman

$\mathcal{I}$n 1967 Raoul Lévy, the producer of, among other films, *And God Created Woman*, *En cas de malheur* and *La Vérité*, committed suicide. He shot himself, escaping from a chaotic business career and the latest of many disastrous love affairs. Just a few weeks earlier he had delivered an epitaph on a style of films, and an actress, that he had helped create: 'The demystification of the stars, due to too much publicity about their private lives, is ruining the box office. There is no longer any mystery about Bardot. The public knows too many intimate things about her life. Bardot sells newspapers and magazines, but she does not sell tickets.'

This was Frankenstein complaining about the behaviour of the monster that he had, if not created, then at least unleashed on the world. It was absurd to complain that there was 'no longer' any mystery about Bardot, when Bardot's subversive power had been to abolish all the mysteries and concealments and artifices of cinematic sex. If Bardot was now plagued by the press, if her private and public personas were indistinguishable to the detriment of each, who was it if not Lévy who had invited this publicity from the beginning, encouraging rumours that the star of *And God Created Woman* was just playing herself, that the love scenes were real? Perhaps his despair was actually a realization that the sexual earthquake represented by Bardot, the overtness of desire and its expression, would only occur once, followed perhaps by a few trivial aftershocks. The phenomenon could be explored and there might be meretricious

attempts to repeat the original, but the revelation, such as it was, could only occur once.

The supposed competition between Jeanne Moreau and Bardot in *Viva Maria!* had probably been non-existent and it was irrelevant within the context of that film. Though not an inspired partnership, they are affable and relaxed together. But as actresses the two of them could not have been more different. Moreau was far from an obviously beautiful woman, and could often look positively plain, yet she is an actress who could always be inspired by subject matter, by a director, a co-star, and be intensely attractive, alive with intelligence and passion. She is the reminder that sex is to do with the mind, a matter of nuance, innuendo, disguise, construction. Her captivating sexuality was as much an expression of thought, of her piercing eyes, as of her body. That is why she could still give an intensely erotic performance as a battered sixty-three-year-old in 1992's *The Old Woman Who Walked in the Sea*.

If Moreau articulated a truth about sexuality, then Bardot articulated another, conflicting, one, which is that sex is just about the body; that at its most basic, it has nothing to do with culture or intelligence or wit, but is something much more primal and that all the sophisticated qualities of a Moreau will lose out to the tanned, supple body, the leonine hair, the unambiguous appetite expressed by the twenty-two-year-old Bardot. There was something unanswerable, in all its egocentricity and thoughtlessness, about that but, as Raoul Lévy may have

Rivalry between Bardot and Jeanne Moreau during the shooting of VIVA MARIA! *was largely a journalistic invention*

come to realize, Moreau's strategy may have been better for those years when the body became a little less supple, when the time spent in the sun took its toll, when the childish expression began to harden.

In 1967 Bardot and Serge Gainsbourg recorded the original version of that kitsch classic, 'Je t'aime moi non plus', an account of sexual congress performed to an incongruous easy-listening accompaniment, with such lines as:

> Tu es la vague, moi l'île nue
> Tu vas, tu vas et tu viens
> Entre mes reins

> (You are the wave, I am the bare island, you go, you go and you come between my loins.)

However, when Gunther Sachs heard the song, he forbade it to be released, which was rather like closing the stable door after a whole herd of stallions had bolted. (Bardot's version was not issued until years later.) Gainsbourg re-recorded the song with his wife, Jane Birkin, and the record was an international hit, much as *And God Created Woman* had been ten years earlier. There were rumours – that went carefully undenied – suggesting that Gainsbourg and Birkin had recorded the song while they were actually having sex. Record stations around the world banned the record, which only encouraged people to buy it to hear the song for themselves.

A last couple of sparks of apparent ambition showed themselves in Bardot's film career. She made a final film, or at least part of a film, for a serious director. During the sixties there was a fashion for portmanteau movies, or *films à sketch*, as they were known in France, in which a feature film would contain three or four stories made by different directors, often very distinguished ones. Alain Delon invited Louis Malle to contribute to *Histories Extraordinaires*, three adaptations of stories by Edgar Allan Poe, along with Roger Vadim and Orson Welles (though, like so many other Welles projects, this came to nothing and the third segment was ultimately directed by Federico Fellini). Malle chose to adapt Poe's remarkable tale, *William Wilson*, about an evil man who is tormented by his double, a man who shares his name. The leading role was taken by Delon and for the minor role of a woman he cheats in a card game, the producers suggested Bardot, whereas Malle was keen to cast a little-known actress who would not overbalance this miniature story. As he later recalled: 'I'd heard that Bardot was away somewhere on a cruise and was so convinced that she wouldn't be available that I said, "Sure, why not?" However, she'd had a row with her boyfriend and come back to Paris, and she said, "Oh, I'd love to work again with Louis and with Alain Delon." So I was stuck.' Malle tried to make the best of it by making Bardot as unlike Bardot as possible, putting her in a dark wig, having her act in an impassive, static style, wearing period costume (the film is set in the nineteenth century) but he still regarded it as 'terrible casting, unforgivable'. The result was quite an impressive film, but it did no good for Bardot's prospects.

Still less was she helped by her next project. At the age of thirty-four, Bardot finally made what could be seen as a Hollywood film. In reality *Shalako* was more

OPPOSITE

A bewigged Bardot and Serge Gainsbourg, with whom she recorded 'Je t'aime moi non plus'

like a simulacrum of a Hollywood movie, a western with British producers, shot in Spain. Bardot was paired with Sean Connery who was having his own image problems, typecast by five earlier appearances as James Bond. The story was about a party of European aristocrats and Washington politicians undertaking an illegal hunting expedition on an Indian reservation in defiance of a treaty signed with the Indians. The lone gunman, Shalako (played by Connery), encounters them as they are attacked and attempts to lead them to safety. This was just the period when, contrary to anything that would have been predicted, the American western was being re-invented and revitalized in Europe. Clint Eastwood, four years older than Bardot with a career on the verge of extinction, was turned into a major star by his work with Sergio Leone in Spain in the mid-sixties and Leone's style continued to be the decisive influence on the westerns Eastwood made in America.

OPPOSITE _____

Malle and Bardot re-united for WILLIAM WILSON: *'terrible casting, unforgiveable'*

Perhaps Bardot was unlucky, or perhaps her heart was no longer in her career. Three times she would venture into this territory, most promisingly in *Viva Maria!*, then with dismal results in *Shalako*, and three years later in one of her last films, *Les Pétroleuses* (*The Legend of Frenchie King*), a truly catastrophic attempt to recreate the style of *Viva Maria!* (this time with Claudia Cardinale as her co-star). In later years she insisted that she had never bothered much about her film career and by this stage she would not have been interested in seeking out the right director for a particular project, nor would she have been qualified to select the right director even if she had been interested. Instead of choosing a European

director on the rise, the producers selected an American director on the slide, Edward Dmytryk, a once significant figure, whose career had never recovered from the shock of having been blacklisted.

Bardot's first leading role in English is an ignominious disaster. Her command of the language is precarious, she was plainly unable to manage any extended speech and even her briefer lines of dialogue are sometimes barely comprehensible. This aspect of the film is enough in itself to explain Bardot's decision not to attempt a career in the United States. And she looks little better than she sounds. It was presumably decided that her long-haired, sun-tanned Saint-Tropez look was inappropriate for a period film but even that would have been better than the straight hair and the mask-like make-up which constrain her as much as the English consonants with which she struggles so unavailingly.

It is a clumsy, muddled film which incidentally conveys some of the unfairness of the film world. Bardot is unimpressive, but no less so than Sean Connery, five years her senior, who also had the advantage of acting in his own language. (The film required a long scrolling text at the beginning in order to explain why it was plausible for a European hunting party in the Wild West to be rescued by a Scottish cowboy.) Bardot has frequently been criticized either as a bad actress or, at best, for her limited range, yet Connery was equally limited. He won an Academy Award for a performance as an Irish-American policeman which he played with his usual Scottish accent. Whatever Bardot had achieved, however she had conducted her career, there would be no *Untouchables* or *Indiana Jones and the Last Crusade* or, for that matter, *In the Line of Fire* or *Unforgiven* (which revived

Clint Eastwood's career, once again) because such roles simply don't exist for women. Bardot invented a new sort of persona for young women; no one has yet done the same thing for older women unwilling to play spinsterish detectives or Mother Courage.

The shooting of *Shalako* only served to emphasize Bardot's apparent lack of ambition. 'First I am a woman,' she told one interviewer, 'and only second an actress. I am *not* like some actresses who only come alive when they are in front of the movie camera. I live when I am not filming.' Insouciance of this kind was a form of challenge when spoken by the twenty-two-year-old Bardot, an affront to less attractive people who needed to work at the craft of acting. Twelve years on it sounded more like a straightforward lack of commitment from a woman who would rather be at a party or a disco. She half-heartedly spoke up for strong directors with the same hollowness with which she might have called for a strong man to tame her for a respectable domestic life: 'I am a better actress if the director takes hold of me and is masterful. I like that. Some people think you have to be old and ugly before they will say you are good. I prefer to be beautiful and not so good.'

It now seemed improbable that a Clouzot would be able to force a great performance out of Brigitte Bardot. She was too well-protected for that. Sean Connery was reputedly appalled by the size of the entourage that arrived at Almería in Spain in her wake. She herself was transported to the location in a white Rolls-Royce driven by a handsome black chauffeur. The car had been grey but she had ordered it to be repainted in order to set off the chauffeur more strikingly.

As ever, she was discontented to be on a film set, especially outside France, as she flirtatiously complained to a journalist: 'In a strange place I am a cat, forever prowling to find a familiar odour and a safe corner. And when I can't find it, I scratch, scratch, scratch.' Her attraction to animals became more obtrusive, to the point of being a distraction from her work. She was always less interested in endangered wild species than in domestic or farm animals that had been abandoned or mistreated, victims of failed relationships. On the set of *Shalako* she adopted a stray dog, as she had in Mexico while making *Viva Maria!*. Considering that nothing was too good for it, she inadvisedly fed it foie gras, which proved to be too rich for a canine constitution weakened by neglect and it promptly died. She then went into mourning and was unable to participate in filming for several days.

For her performance in *Shalako* even to have reached the level of competence would have required intense dedication in order to improve her English and breathe life into a moribund role. Instead, she seemed determined to prove that anything was more important to her than the business of acting. She had an affair with Stephen Boyd, an old co-star from *Les bijoutiers du clair de lune*. She had still been in love with her husband, she later recalled: 'But when I had to go on location in the backwoods of Spain, my lover couldn't follow me. And when I didn't see him for three months, well, I found another one.' She was constantly at parties and clubs or posing for photographers. Whatever her stamina as a partygoer or a dancer, in *Shalako* she looked for the first time stolid, even old, and the film was dismissed by the

OPPOSITE _____

SHALAKO (1968): the sexual chemistry between Bardot and Sean Connery fizzled and went out

critics and failed completely at the box office.

Bardot's marriage to Gunther Sachs had been rendered meaningless by a string of affairs but, though they were divorced at the end of 1969, he always spoke admiringly of her, particularly paying tribute to her high intelligence. He praised her most highly as a writer (the vividness of her letters has often been commented on by close friends), as a conversationalist, as a dancer, and almost incidentally as an actress.

There was intense public interest in her future. Even John Updike, in his poem about a holiday in France, *Farewell to the Shopping District of Antibes*, concluded with the couplet: 'JOURNAUX will ask, though I'm away, UN AUTRE MARI POUR B.B.?' But Bardot herself, now in her mid-thirties and divorced for the third time, insisted that marriage was not for her and openly adopted the role of a sexually predatory man with an especial taste for young men. Jane Fonda, as the wife of Roger Vadim, got to know Bardot around this time and praised her as a woman who didn't talk feminism but put a version of it into practice: 'she kicked out any man she was tired of and invited in any man she wanted, she lived like a man.' The historian of France, Theodore Zeldin, has pointed out that this view was based on a misunderstanding, part of an attempt to avoid the complexities of French society. Even when she acted in the fashion praised by Fonda, this was living like a very old-fashioned sort of rake. If Bardot's example proved anything, it was that there was nothing simple about following natural impulses, however apparently pleasurable such an existence might seem.

The Rabelaisian Bardot was looked on with admiration, awe or disapproval. It was around this time that she was voted the most popular pin-up by French teenagers, an accolade she greeted with the statement: 'They like me because they sense I will never settle down, that, like them, I am completely available.' Once a subversive figure, she now found herself curiously in tune with at least some sections of society, a living propagandist on behalf of a life based on guilt-free, no-questions-asked sexual activity, with no pretence about love, fidelity, let alone marriage or children. One of Bardot's biographers, Glenys Roberts, describes a dinner party given by Fonda and Vadim at their farmhouse in St Ouen, twenty-five miles from Paris, at which Bardot and Warren Beatty were present. In an example of the fabled charm that has reputedly won over so many glamorous women, Beatty complimented Fonda on the meal but 'looking at Bardot meaningfully, then said he knew something which tasted even better. Vadim, who was very drunk, then made the vulgar comment: "In that area Jane is not quite in Brigitte's class." While Jane was beside herself with fury, Brigitte was far from displeased. She had been paid a compliment, she liked vulgarity, and she could console herself that there were holes in everyone's marriage.'

This rabidly rutting Bardot became almost a character of folklore, sidling up to beautiful young men on the dance floor. Marguerite Duras had evoked the ritual a few years earlier: 'When a man attracts her, Bardot goes straight to him. Nothing stops her. It does not matter if she is in a café, at home or staying with friends. She goes off with him on the spot without a glance at the man she is leaving. In the evening perhaps she will come back – or perhaps not.' Once ensnared, the man would be taken to her legendary bachelor apartment in Paris (spinster apartment doesn't have quite the appropriate ring to it)

*Brigitte Bardot: I want to
be alone*

RIGHT

*Bardot spotted in her
characteristic late-sixties
habitat: the disco dancefloor*

or to La Madrague in Saint-Tropez where he would be installed for a few days or weeks until one day he would get out of bed to find his suitcase packed and standing in the doorway, a cab outside with the meter running. One, it is said, was an English teenager, in Paris for a brief holiday, who found himself ensconced in Bardot's lair until his mother came over to La Manche and rescued him.

Perhaps a couple of weeks of this was enough. One of the anonymous lovers spoke of the experience:

'She is so beautiful, so extraordinarily desirable at every moment of her life, all hours of the day and night, whatever her mood, whether she is gay, sad or bored. She is so desirable that life with her becomes an inferno of desire.

'One cannot hesitate to approach her, to pester her, to live in terror of losing her. I think all her men have exhausted her patience. I, too ... it's enough to drive a man mad. I *was* mad throughout the period we lived together.'

Yet at the same time Bardot became another archetype, representing the impossibility of a life devoted entirely to pleasure. We take a voyeuristic pleasure in contemplating a life like Bardot's and are willing to admire it in fragments, just as the men were willing to experience it briefly, but we also want to be reassured that our own normal lives – with families, children, responsibilities – embody the true values. There is little doubt that Bardot's hedonistic, self-indulgent existence was isolated, arduous and not always much fun. As Theodore Zeldin puts it: 'Being natural was in fact very hard work.

It made her profoundly lonely. She used to need constant company at the height of her fame ... She had great difficulty in coping with her natural impulses or making sense of them.' Marguerite Duras interpreted Bardot's sexual voracity as a form of fear, attracting men like a Circean sorceress to quench her own fear of finding herself alone in her bed:

The sleep of her lover is her sleep. I don't say that this is selfishness, no. I'm saying something quite different – that Bardot is a mythological being even in her own eyes.

Each of her lovers is in some degree a night-duty man, the person who will enable her to avoid sleeping alone. The curious thing, nevertheless, is that although all have been warned of the danger of loving her nobody has yet recoiled.

The wild overstatement of this – the only danger from an affair with Bardot in those pre-Aids days was the risk of dropping your suitcase on your foot as she kicked you out – suggests that Bardot had become the focus for thoughts that were really about sex as a whole at a time when sex was being considered the centre of an ideology, a panacea, a way of dissolving old structures and taboos. If Beauvoir had welcomed this connection – sex today, society tomorrow – then Duras wanted to bring back the dark side of sex, to insist that sex can be as much an expression of fear, violence, betrayal as of love or liberation.

Bardot herself was equally torn, as she was about her film career. Her carefree attitude to loving and leaving, like her lack of concern for her career or the mechanics of filmmaking, could be an expression of freedom. But then there were the breakdowns and the suicide attempts suggesting that the detachment might have other, less healthy, causes. And just as she would look back on her film career as largely a waste in which she had no interest, so she would pronounce her personal life to be a series of failures. She would later tell Françoise Sagan in an interview: 'I am a woman who has undoubtedly made a success of her career but certainly not of her private life. Let's say someone who is incomplete.'

Just as she had balanced the respectability of her family against the charming chaotic bohemianism of

Vadim, so she had always been able to keep her life and career in uneasy balance. While filming she would insist that she didn't care about the cinema and that what really mattered to her was living. Yet her private life, saturated by media attention, was entirely sacrificed to the demands of her public career. Relationships, even that with her child, were temporary, something to be dropped while she ran off to make a film, or to start another relationship.

This balance broke down as it became painfully clear that her career was in terminal decline. There are criticisms that can be made of Bardot here. She never made any serious attempt to develop her image, to play an older woman, to explore the dilemmas of a woman entering middle age, in the way that she had once made films scrutinizing the conflicts that could destroy a free-spirited young girl. Yet the simple fact is that the careers of star actresses always go into decline sooner or later.

Jane Fonda was frequently praised as an actress who grew old gracefully on screen yet her last significant hit was *On Golden Pond* (1981) when she was only forty-four. For those stars especially celebrated for their glamour, the decline is traditionally more like a collapse. The most dignified are those who find something else to do, becoming a stage actor once again, like Katharine Hepburn; becoming a stage singer, like Judy Garland or Marlene Dietrich; or ostentatiously retiring, like Greta Garbo. But by comparison with legendary actresses like Rita Hayworth, Betty Hutton, Veronica Lake and Hedy Lamarr, Bardot managed her decline with dignity. The ignominy was brief and, a little tardily, Bardot acted decisively in concluding that enough was enough.

Looking back, Roger Vadim recalled that when his first wife announced her retirement in the early seventies, most people hadn't taken her seriously: 'But I knew she was sincere. She was unable to become, even on screen, a real grown-up person with real adult problems. She hasn't betrayed the little Brigitte. She said goodbye and bowed out while there was still time.'

Vadim modestly omitted to mention his own part in this decision, which was almost as significant as it had been in making her a star, seventeen years earlier. In 1973, after a series of failures, Bardot was re-united with Vadim to star in *Don Juan ou Et si Don Juan était une femme* (*Don Juan or if Don Juan Were a Woman*) under his direction. The title at least suggested something potentially interesting. Whatever his shortcomings as a writer and director when he attempted his cinematic debut, Vadim had been able to capture something startlingly new and fresh about his wife. Perhaps he would now be able to portray the life that Bardot had been leading during her

thirties and have something to say about this life ruthlessly dedicated to personal sexual fulfilment.

But it would have required a different sort of director to make an honest film about Brigitte Bardot as she approached forty, a director with a sense of irony, of time passing, of proportion. Vadim's *Don Juan* is not merely a pathetic collusion with a struggle to deny that Bardot was growing old, it was also clumsily attempting to follow in the wake of fashions that the pair of them had once arrogantly dictated. To the extent that a coherent plot can be extracted from this farrago, Bardot plays a woman who believes herself to be the re-incarnation of the famous Spanish lover. She recounts her recent affairs to her cousin, a priest, with whom she then has sex before being murdered by another lover, a politician, whose life and career she has destroyed by exposing his hypocrisy. Though Bardot may have anticipated the sixties, she never seemed quite at home in that decade. She was a woman who looked best when in slight rebellion with her wardrobe, the wild hair contrasting with the tight skirts or tailored suits. In the kaftans and loose dresses she was photographed in during the late sixties, she was starting to lose her edge, looking blurred and woozy. Not many people looked good in the trouser suits, high-heeled boots, the sweaters with wide leather belts of the early seventies, and with Bardot the effect is almost of drag, as if she were dressing up in somebody else's clothes.

Though there is a hardening around the eyes, the admirable condition of her body is in itself a convincing case for Bardot's regime of, as she claimed, taking no exercise and eating and drinking whatever she felt like, but it simply is not what it once had been. Even in her

OPPOSITE

A veritable cornucopia of early-seventies costume and bric-a-brac, and Bardot is in there somewhere

LEFT

Worn, wrinkled — and that's just the dress. Bardot was never at home in the seventies

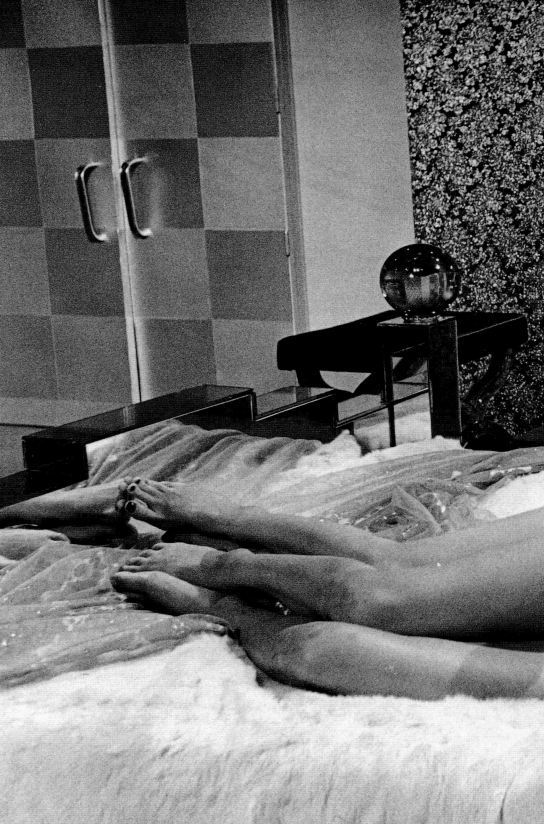

Bardot and Jane Birkin in a tastefully designed scene from Don Juan *(1973). Even the doors don't fit together properly*

worst, tattiest films of the fifties there was a blatant unanswerability about her attractions. In *Une Parisienne* it seems entirely plausible that if she chose to proposition a visiting monarch on a state visit (played by that suavest of leading men, Charles Boyer) he would run off with her, risking the destruction of everything just because of her irresistibility. In *Don Juan* she is like an old boxer who can move around the ring in ways superficially reminiscent of his glory days but without the punch that once made him a champion.

Bardot is scarcely to be blamed for this. Her only crime was to grow old. The truly dismaying failure of intelligence and sensibility is on the part of Roger Vadim. *Don Juan* is an appallingly incompetent film, garishly ugly in design and ludicrously scripted. In *And God Created Woman* sex itself was news. By 1973 the sixties had already gone sour, it had all been done, sex on screen had become a cliché, sexual liberation was a familiar subject and people had long since moved on to consider the possible costs, whether 'liberation' was necessarily the right word. For Beauvoir in 1959, sex itself, stripped of illusion, was intrinsically a political, subversive act. After Haight-Ashbury, Charles Manson and Altamont, the dark side of the Love generation had been revealed. Eden looked different now and it was impossible to be uncomplicatedly innocent about sex.

Like an ageing rocker dutifully recycling the hits, Vadim was incapable of a new response except for the tired variations on the old theme. There is something sad and desperate about the lukewarm bed scene pairing Bardot with Jane Birkin, not because it's about sadness and desperation itself – if only it were – but because of what it tells us about Vadim himself, and his alienated

imagination. By his own account (and hers), he was only fully aware of Bardot's erotic power when he saw it vicariously, in public and through other's eyes. He has said that he reacted to the failures of his marriage with Jane Fonda first by having affairs with other women and then by bringing some of them back to share their bed. (There is a squalid little episode described by John Phillips, one of The Mamas and the Papas, in his memoirs in which Vadim despatches him and Warren Beatty upstairs to join Fonda in bed like some over-anxious host dispensing sherry to his guests.) *Don Juan* is like the final terrible act in a parable about the failings of the erotic imagination and its masturbatory decay and falling away. He puts Bardot in bed with Birkin in the spirit that a drug addict needs an ever-increasing dose in order to elicit the same effect, and he is now doing it with performers who are palpably unengaged for an audience who have seen it all before. *Don Juan* has the production values of pornography, the lack of any sense of a real world, its dehumanized quality, the abstracted performances, everything except the seamy sexual extremity at its centre.

Vadim would continue to produce intermittent films, trading on his reputation with *Night Games* (1980) and, in 1987, using the title *And God Created Woman* for an entirely different story. He wrote a couple of versions of his memoirs, devoting large sections of them to his famous companions.

Bardot made one more film, a medieval comedy catchily titled *L'Histoire très bonne et très joyeuse de Colinot Trousse-Chemise* (*Colinot, the Skirt Puller-upper*) which was never shown outside France, and drew the sensible conclusion. She could still have earned reasonable fees for films but she was no longer any sort of box-office draw and she had not had a worthy role since *Viva Maria!* eight years previously. She was offered the lead in *Someone is Killing the Great Chefs of Europe* but turned it down and it is significant that the actress who finally played the role, Jacqueline Bisset, was fully ten years younger. Bardot announced her retirement and since then she has not shown the slightest hint of being tempted to act: 'The myth of BB is finished,' she said. 'Perhaps in five years people will have forgotten me, maybe not. I will be forty-five. I'll be able to live like everyone else.'

ABOVE ──────────────

The funeral of Louis Bardot in 1975. He had survived to see his daughter's entire film career

Animals

Bardot grew up with animals — in an urban sort of way. She was not interested in seeking out wildlife or studying any of the natural sciences. She never lived on a working farm and hence did not experience animals as a part of a process. Her mother had a poodle while Brigitte herself as a young girl had a cat called Crocus and some birds. Vadim knew of his wife's predilection and in 1953, when she had pulled out of the Hollywood contract offered her by Warner Brothers, he gave her a cocker spaniel, Clown, as a form of compensation.

Her commitment to the rights of animals was not entirely consistent — she was horrified years later when she watched *Une Parisienne* and saw herself wrapped in an ocelot coat. Such indulgences were routine in those pre-Green movement days. She caused more alarm when in the seventies she allowed a photograph of herself in a fur coat to be used in the 'Blackgama, What Becomes a Legend Most?' advertising campaign.

During her film career she began to accumulate animals which had been abandoned or which she had rescued from being slaughtered or from the abuse of their cruel owners. La Madrague, her home in Saint-Tropez, stood on a small area of land and was an impractical habitat for the menagerie she installed there. Much of her time was spent feeding its inhabitants or clearing up their droppings. After the birth of her son Nicolas, in 1960,

she bought an old farm twenty miles from Paris at Bazoches, near Versailles, where she could keep not just cats, dogs and hens but donkeys, horses, sheep and goats.

She came to present her retirement as also an escape from humanity itself. She claimed a particular identification with beleaguered beasts because she knew what it was like to be hunted down, to feel that she had been caught as prey in the sights of a predator: 'The photographers didn't want to kill me but they did kill something in me. They focus on you from far away and they steal something of your soul.'

Now that she had the time, she could devote her energy towards saving animals on a properly organized basis. In 1976 she began her famous campaign against the slaughter of baby seals in northern Canada and in the following year she flew out to the ice to protest on the spot: 'It was horrible. I'd been used to travelling in incredible luxury: first-class tickets and suites in the best hotels. And suddenly I found myself in the cold in this rickety plane, being insulted when I landed and nobody taking me seriously. I was refused meals by the Canadians and thrown out of the single inn in Blanc-Sablon.' She always spoke vividly about the slaughter itself, which became her touchstone for human exploitation of animal suffering: 'The ice was red. I saw it from the plane, streaked with red for miles and miles and strewn with tiny carcasses. They kill them with iron hooks, you know, little two-week-old seals, defenceless little balls of fur and life and love. They skin them on the spot and you

can see the little heart still beating in the bloody mass that remains. And later the blood congeals and you remember the stench all your life.'

In June of 1976 she launched the Brigitte Bardot Foundation for the Protection of Animals, a charitable organization which was run with the help of her new partner, Alain Bougrain-Dubourg, a well-known maker of nature programmes for French television, and ten years her junior. Those who doubted the depth of Bardot's commitment to environmental politics, with all its complexity and bureaucracy, were partially vindicated by the Foundation's troubled progress. Though there were other helpers, the success of the venture depended almost entirely on the personality of its founder and she was strangely capricious in her contributions. She refused even to speak at its highly publicized launch and was frequently unwilling to make use of her own fame, sometimes refusing to be photographed in return for large donations. One aspiring biographer offered her a percentage of potential royalties to be donated to the animal charity of her choice and was informed by Bardot's agent: 'Brigitte isn't interested in all the animals in the world. She has her own and that is enough.' What was the point of giving up her film career and then maintaining the ludicrous intrusions that had driven her out of it? On the other hand was it not her responsibility to do what she could in order to achieve her goals?

Bardot has never been short of analysts and the subject of her commitment to animals proved irresistible. She liked animals because she identified with their suffering, it was speculated. She had been let down so often by

OPPOSITE —————

La Madrague, Saint-Tropez in 1982: Bardot at home with guitar and at least four dogs

men that she was desperate to find a form of relationship that was based on authentic trust and loyalty uncontaminated by notions of fame and reputation, and this she found with her stray cats and dogs. As Bardot herself had said: 'People will betray your secrets, your friendship and your love. But animals will never deceive you. If you love them, they love you back.' It was just a whim, said others, the traditional sentimental attitude that actresses generally have to cute animals here elevated into an entire way of life. Certainly Bardot has never shown much concern for the larger questions of ecology, nor has she stuck to a rigorous conception of animal rights. She has responded to individual cases of animal suffering on their merits as she saw them at the time. She has at various times advised eskimos to stop eating the whale meat on which their whole culture depends, and condemned the slaughter of animals according to the dictates of Jewish and Islamic law, while persisting in eating meat herself, offering a defence likely to enrage vegetarians and nutritionists equally: 'I don't eat much, anyway, and very little meat. But without any meat, it made me want to eat pasta and potatoes, which is not good for the figure, is it?'

To anybody born after 1960, Bardot was less famous as an actress than as an animal rights activist, not so much participating in a single sustained campaign but rather in a series of individual struggles, a politics of impulse, that was as likely to manifest itself on the spur of the moment, rescuing a mangy dog or an aged horse in a local lane as in the courts or the European Parliament. In December 1979 she joined with the French League against Vivisection to sue a Professor Henri Sarles for his alleged cruelty in carrying out experiments on dogs. The case was thrown out of court. In 1983 she had a slander case brought against her by a Saint-Tropez florist, Madame Odette Giraud. She demanded over £750 in damages after Bardot had stormed into her shop and shouted at her: 'Anyone who clubs her cat to death is a dirty bitch and a criminal.' Giraud countered in court that it was in fact her son who had executed the animal but she lost her case. The following year Bardot's status as an institution, now the respectable embodiment of wholesome French sex, in a time when sex was once again becoming a dirty word, and as a doughty campaigner as well, was recognized when she was awarded La Légion d'honneur.

In 1987 she sold off many of her more valuable possessions at the leading Paris auction house, Salle Drouot, in order to raise money for the struggle. These were the sort of things to which she had never been much attached: photographs, a guitar, a watch, her wedding dress from her first marriage, and then some more expensive gifts from Gunther Sachs, including three matching but differently coloured bracelets he had given her for their wedding and a single diamond that alone was valued at £100,000. Then in her mid-fifties, she stirringly claimed: 'I have dedicated my beauty and my youth to the human race. Now I am giving my wisdom and my experience, and the best of myself, to the cause of animals.' It may be argued that the human race got the better end of the deal but the auction remarkably raised more than £300,000, demonstrating that 'Bardolatry' survived, almost a decade and a half since she had last made a film.

Her life in the courts continued. In August 1988 she sued *VSD*, a French magazine, which had alleged that cats can get Aids, thus, Bardot claimed, spreading panic among pet owners. The following year she herself was sued by her neighbour at La Madrague, an industrialist called Jean-Pierre Manivet, who had asked Bardot to look after his donkey, Charly, while he was on holiday. Bardot took such alarm at Charly's eagerness to mate, either with her own donkey, Cornichoo, or with one of her frail elderly mares, rescued from a life of toil elsewhere, that she had him castrated by a local vet. This caused fury to Manivet and great amusement in the press but Bardot proved herself once more an effective litigant and Manivet ended up being fined 20,000 francs.

Now in her mid-fifties, she benefited from the rise of the Green movement throughout Europe and gained more influence, especially through a television programme, *SOS Animaux*, that she began to present on French television. At the same time, this role as a roving animal ambassador inevitably attracted controversy as

ABOVE

A signed Bardot portrait, sold to raise money for her wildlife foundation

well. She had no interest in any cause that didn't involve either animals or local politics in Saint-Tropez. She would protest to the President of Rwanda about the alleged slowness in hunting down the killers of Dian Fossey, because Fossey had become a heroine of Bardot's through her campaign to save the country's gorillas (though Fossey herself had been controversial for what was seen by some as her arrogant disregard for local people and culture). When Bardot announced in July 1990 that she would go to South Africa, it was in order to protest at the 'useless and barbaric' slaughter of seals for aphrodisiacs and pet food, which must have given some light relief to the beleaguered President de Klerk, who at the time had one or two other issues to deal with that may have seemed more pressing than the ingredients of domestic pet food. To some there was an offensive lack of proportion in her protests. During the Gulf War she complained about the sea birds covered in oil. She criticized the Soviet Union, citing 'the gulags which the Russians have built especially for the extermination of baby seals.'

Later in the summer of 1990, Bardot commented on the fate of the bullfighter, Julio Robles, who had been critically injured in the ring at Béziers in Languedoc, in terms that did little to endear her to Robles' family: 'People forget that the bull who injured him was sacrificed, despite having proved itself stronger. It should have been saved. There is no code of honour any more towards animals.' She appealed directly to Felipe Gonzalez, the prime minister of Spain, to abolish the sport of bullfighting entirely. A couple of years later she would angrily denounce Gérard Dépardieu for trying his hand at bullfighting during a break in the shooting of his

film about Columbus, *1492: Conquest of Paradise*, perhaps forgetting that she had done the same thing on screen, to demonstrate her character's impulsiveness and courage, in *Les Bijoutiers du claire de lune*, thirty years earlier.

She was not always in tune with ordinary French people. In 1985 she led a protest against the shooting of *les tourterelles*, an annual event when these turtle doves pass through France while migrating from the Sahara. The hunters, almost uniformly poor, rural people, organized and defeated her protest, with the tacit encouragement of local police, who refused to intervene, largely because the protesters were seen as a rich Paris clique out of touch with the provincial traditions that are so important a part of the French psyche.

An occasional failure of this kind notwithstanding, it now seemed as if Bardot's image had changed decisively. On the tenth anniversary of her retirement from films she complained about the resentment she had always aroused: 'Women really hated me. They thought I stole men, ruined their lives and then threw them away. But it is a matter of pride for me that I never stole anybody who was not available.' In that same year she was voted the most admired woman in France, in a poll organized by the magazine, *Paris Match*. She now seemed to have become a reassuring figure who could be relied on to denounce the excesses of the age. She was against open permissiveness: 'Yes, for me love needs mystery, secrecy and silence. It is a private, very rich and complex affair, but at the same time very simple. The more I hear about all those perversions, the less I want to make love. I think that exhibitionism is shame. Repressed but shame.' She was

OPPOSITE ————

Protesting at the hunting of turtle doves, one of her less popular campaigns

Bardot at twenty-one: a classic image by Philippe Halsman

opposed to feminism: 'Women may be liberated, but look at them. They are unhappy, alone, divorced and abandoned. A woman is a woman and even now, at the end of the twentieth century, that means she should stay with her family, with her home, and with her husband.' As for the cinema, it was a 'profession of idiots'. This was what people wanted to hear, the prodigal daughter grown old. An interviewer from the left-wing newspaper, *Libération*, told her that she was 'loved by millions of people'. Bardot had been vaguely and inconsequentially talking for many years about writing her memoirs and in 1990 she signed a contract with Jacqueline Onassis (of the American publishers, Doubleday), a woman with a reputation for persuading reclusive celebrities like Michael Jackson to produce books.

In 1991 the Philippe Halsman portrait of the young Bardot jumping playfully in the air, the most charming photograph of her ever taken, was used as a poster for Air France, confirming that she was now officially one of the great French assets, the soft, female symbol, curves and smiles, to be contrasted with the metallically phallic Eiffel Tower. She had been the symbol of the guilt-free sex of the future. Now she was the equally tantalizing symbol of guilt-free, and safe, sex of the past. In March of the same year, when *Esquire* launched a new British edition, they put Bardot on the cover of their first issue, an appropriate gesture for the magazine which had commissioned Simone de Beauvoir's essay on the actress more than twenty years before.

On 3 April 1992 Bardot won a special United Nations environment award for her work to protect animals. It seemed, miraculously, that she had finally killed the myth and reached that state she had spoken of shortly

LEFT

Brigitte Bardot, the all-purpose sexual icon

after her retirement: 'I am dreaming of the time when I can do things which amuse me and for which I alone am responsible. I will no longer be a beautiful object but a human being.' But at the moment of her apparent acceptance as a revered figure approaching old age it became clear that the conflict between her public and private lives was as alive as ever and always would be.

Since the breakdown of her marriage to Sachs, Bardot had been involved with a series of younger men, less famous than herself (though how many men could she have met who would be more famous?). Before meeting Bougrain-Dubourg she lived with a young Czech sculptor, Miroslav Brozcek. Apart from her activities on behalf of animals, she lived a quiet life and, when asked, admitted to just half a dozen or so really close friends: her ex-husbands, Gunther Sachs and Roger Vadim; her sister, Mijanou; her son, Nicolas, with whom she had been re-united when he became an adult; her producer, Christine Gouze-Renal and her agent Olga Horstig (though she had retired as an actress, Bardot still appeared in advertisements and represented beauty products which demanded less of her time).

Apart from appearances in court and at demonstrations, Bardot now featured in newspapers mainly on her birthday. There is no film star in history, with the possible exception of Shirley Temple, for whom the passing of time has seemed a matter of such importance. She was notorious for having attempted suicide on the evening that she completed her first quarter-century and from then on the significant anniversaries were always a subject of widespread attention. In the increasingly rare interviews that were granted, she – who had been so flagrantly, sinfully young – was asked how it felt to grow

old. Other actresses, especially in America, have made desperate, usually self-deceptive attempts to shore their bodies up against the effects of time by having parts of their body removed or tightened but, outside the unworthy final films of her career, Bardot was generally unblinking about the process of ageing. She contemplated her body's decay with the grim helplessness of someone watching a great fresco cracking and being irreversibly lost. At forty-one, an age when most people consider themselves to be still acceptably young, she was asked by Françoise Sagan if she was afraid of dying. After all, to imagine the heedless young Bardot ever reaching middle age would once have seemed as unthinkable, and therefore just about the same, as death, in the spirit of Pete Townshend's 'hope I die before I get old' (in The Who's 'My Generation'). She denied that she was afraid, but her vivid language suggested otherwise: 'What is atrocious for me is that my body doesn't disintegrate immediately when I die and that afterwards there is the resting place, embalming, smelling … burial.'

OPPOSITE

Bardot celebrating her forty-fifth birthday with kaftan and current boyfriend, Miroslav Brozcek

The central limitation of the rock and roll youth culture was precisely that: its preoccupation with youth and its perspectives and attributes. 'It's better to burn out than to fade away,' wrote Neil Young (in 'Rust Never Sleeps'), but in an interview given shortly before he was murdered, John Lennon said that this was childish and of course it was better to fade away. For most participants it was a dilemma that was impossible to solve.

Bardot talked of her new resilience, of the good friends she was attached to, her animals, and her three cosy homes: 'I like to be able to touch the ceilings,' she eloquently put it. But on the eve of her forty-ninth birth-day she was left by Bougrain-Dubourg, her lover of six years. Gunther Sachs had once commented to her on her need for company: 'Brigitte, you are like a beautiful sail-ing boat in the middle of a bay. But if there isn't anyone around to blow the sails, you don't move.' Late that night a stranger found her wandering into the sea having taken an overdose of tablets.

Interviewed a year later by *Paris Match* she was raging about the idea of being fifty, and could be seen to be dis-concertingly shattering our comforting illusions about age just the way that she had about youth when she was in her early twenties. We like to believe that there is something unsat-isfactory and unformed about youth, but as a young woman she asserted that life was simply more fun if you were young and beautiful, and sex was better if it could be enjoyed with-out responsibility. Our next illusion, if that is what it is, is that we improve and mature as we grow older, that there are gains with the grey hairs and wrinkles. What Bardot alarmingly stated was that this wasn't true, that old age was a process of loss and disintegration which was unbearable to contemplate too directly. What was it like to be fifty? 'It makes me want to puke! People who say, "It's marvellous to be fifty," must be mad! I've got the temperament of a young girl. I dance, I play the gui-tar, and I feel as if I'm sixteen, but my face doesn't fit … It's not the end of youth which gets me. It's the begin-ning of all the problems with one's health – I who have never been ill.' And in another ten years? 'It will be worse. I'll be sixty, and prefer not to think about that.'

OPPOSITE

Bardot discussing life as a forty-year-old on French television with Françoise Sagan

The illness she was referring to was breast cancer, for which she required an operation in 1984.

There is something bracingly admirable about Bardot's refusal to talk about the beauty of growing old, the value of experience. For some time, in her later twenties and early thirties, perhaps, she looked younger than her age but then the years in the intense Mediterranean sun took their toll and her appearance changed rapidly during her fifties, a process she com-mented on vividly, as if on the vandalism of a revered French monument: 'It is terrible, obscene to think that one will one day look like an old map of France.' It was a pity that there could be no possibility of all this passion finding expression on the big screen, of a film which could be as shocking about middle age as *And God Created Woman* had been about youth, but it would have required a different director than Vadim, still peddling his tired, mindless, hedonism. What would have been needed was a director like Louis Malle or Bertrand Tavernier who could make a film *about* Vadim and his tragic, futile cult of youthful sexuality. Would Bardot now be willing to be scrutinized by the camera as honestly as Jane Birkin so movingly and unsparingly had been in Tavernier's *Daddy nostalgie* (*These Foolish Things*), in which she played Dirk Bogarde's middle-aged daughter. Certainly Bardot now looked far better than those awkward years in her forties when she was visibly losing the battle to appear as if she were in her twenties. She now had a severe, wrinkled elegance, which gave her the air of a Jeanne Moreau, or of the intellectual women who had written so shrewdly about her, Simone de Beauvoir or Marguerite Duras.

After the break-up with Bougrain-Dubourg, Bardot spent much of her fifties unattached. Then, in the

summer of 1992 Bardot visited Norway where her son Nicolas now lived, married to a Norwegian, and met her two granddaughters for the first time. While she was there, on 16 August, she secretly married her companion, the businessman, Bernard d'Ormale, who at fifty-one was seven years her junior. In various ways he might have seemed an ideal husband for Bardot as she entered old age. He was good-looking, intelligent, intensely private, with a highly successful career of his own. He was described as a 'great animal lover and a keen supporter of animal rights', a crucial qualification for a consort of Brigitte Bardot. He was also a leading member of the French National Front, the extreme right-wing party led by Jean-Marie Le Pen, which had made striking gains in the South of France, not least in d'Ormale's home town of Nice, where he was the dominant National Front politician.

OPPOSITE

Bardot in 1987, becoming accepted, even admired, as an elder stateswoman — but not for long

News of the marriage caused great shock, not least because Bardot was assumed to be, if anything, a supporter of the political left. This was an assumption frequently made about young actors and pop stars, largely because they were considered to be rebels, yet in reality these people were generally classic examples of self-made people and were basically right-wing, whether they knew it or not. Their isolated status made them more attuned to the ethos of the extreme right, with its worship of strong leaders, than the egalitarianism, bureaucracy and party discipline of the left. Hence the quasi-fascist outbursts by Eric Clapton and David Bowie in the mid-seventies which caused such alarm and resulted in the birth of the Rock Against Racism movement in Britain.

People started to wonder whether there wasn't something fascistic, or fascist-like, about the worship of youth and beauty that Bardot had stood for. She had never been much of a democrat, or spoken in favour of tolerance and pluralism. Her unarticulated doctrine of liberation could be seen as an assertion of unbridled personal power and she became no more tolerant of fleshly frailty as she grew old: 'People asked me to undress because I was beautiful,' she said at the time of her retirement, 'and being beautiful and young I was happy to do so. I think it is disgusting for the old and ugly to reveal themselves with all their bulges and shortcomings as they do every summer in Saint-Tropez.' An idyll of sexual freedom — if you are beautiful enough to deserve it.

There have long been associations between extreme right-wing organizations and some green movements because of the notions they share about the organic society, the soil, the distrust of the market, the value of rural life when set against the life of the city. Even before she had met d'Ormale, some of Bardot's supporters were starting to worry about where she was being carried, unthinkingly, as they believed, by her convictions. In 1989 she gave an interview to a right-wing publication, *National Hebdo*, in which she said that 'everything had to be done to stop an infamous ritual carried out by those who have invaded our country and do not even have the decency to respect our laws.' And in her TV programme, *SOS Animaux*, she called on the agriculture minister, Henri Nallet, to outlaw ritual slaughtering by Muslims and Jews.

Some of her fellow-supporters of animal rights may have shared her disquiet over the methods by which animals were killed according to some religious laws, but

RIGHT

Bardot with her fourth husband, Bernard d'Ormale, businessman and National Front activist

most would have hesitated to denounce publicly, for example, the ritual slaughter of sheep at Aid-el-Kebir, the end of the Islamic Ramadan fast, as a 'revolting practice'. Worse still, she delivered this diatribe, in which she argued that human ought not to be permitted to 'put animals to such cruel and barbarous torture in the name of religion,' in *Présence*, the National Front magazine. If there were any doubts about her irresponsibility, she attacked the French government for supporting the spread of Islam in France, thus linking her views on animals to the general racist claims about foreigners that were being articulated with such success by Le Pen.

After her marriage, Bardot's new respectable status seemed instantly in doubt. In September 1992 she dropped out of *SOS Animaux*. In November her stomach was pumped after an overdose of tranquillizers. It was later reported that she had been depressed after hearing of eleven sheep who had starved to death. At a time when racist attacks were mounting all over Europe, Bardot's exclusive devotion to the maltreatment of animals began to seem less like a charming foible. The Brigitte Bardot Foundation was one of France's richest charities but within a year it suffered a two-thirds fall in donations because of its perceived association with the extreme political right. Unauthorized photographers who had once used their long lenses to capture BB sunbathing in the nude, now caught her with her husband enjoying Le Pen's hospitality on his yacht. The suspicion that Bardot would become a symbol to be manipulated by a man, seemed to be confirmed when the director of Bardot's animal sanctuary, Liliane Sujansky, was sacked and replaced by Stéphane Charpentier, an acquaintance of her husband's. The haemorrhaging funds led to a financial crisis in her foundation, and to service the debts she even had to give up ownership of La Madrague, though she is still permitted to live there.

In December 1993 she gave an interview to *Libération* in an attempt to repair the damage. She lamented that she had spent seven years on her own, 'moping along', and that it had been her bad luck to fall in love with a man in the National Front: 'He takes care of the politics; I look after the animals,' she explained and she conceded that for her the National Front was 'too extremist'. But if this turning-away from her animal charity continued, she would have to choose between d'Ormale and the animals and that would mean they would have to separate, 'and I think it would be unfair for me to have to end my life alone. It's the demonization of love.' The one-time sexual propagandist, who had turned her relationship with animals into a basis for political activism, now seemed chillingly blind to the link between personal relationships and public responsibility.

There had been a short period where Bardot seemed in danger of becoming a figure viewed with general public affection but this was now firmly in the past. In January 1994 she received death threats after her appearance on the French television programme, *Sacrée Soir*, during which she denounced the practice of eating horsemeat. She introduced a film showing various equine slaughterhouses, proclaiming that horses suffered dreadfully when they were killed: 'The horse is also an extraordinary symbol and is not made for our dinner plates.' Undeterred by the police guards who were assigned to her, Bardot open letter to Jean Puech, the French agriculture minister, demanding that the consumption of horsemeat be made illegal. Two butchers from Noisy-le-Sec, near Paris, pressed charges against her because of her claim that horsemeat was unhealthy.

There is nothing settled about the prospect of Bardot at sixty. The signs of her becoming a revered elder stateswoman proved to be as illusory as all of the other hints throughout her life that she might relapse into respectability. She is discontented with growing old, her private and public life are disastrously intermingled and she has shown once more that she has the ability to outrage decent opinion, just as she did almost forty years ago.

In one of her more defiant moments, when she was all of thirty-five, Bardot contended: 'I cannot imagine myself at sixty. I am Brigitte Bardot, and that Brigitte Bardot, the one I see in the magazines and the newspapers, the one who is up on the movie screen, that Brigitte Bardot will never be sixty. Don't you agree?'

We are the first generation who can contemplate people who have grown old but remain young on screen. The difference in age between me and Lillian Gish is roughly that between Bernard Shaw and John Keats, yet all that Shaw could ever see of Keats's appearance was a couple of unreliable drawings. I have seen Lillian Gish as she was at nineteen in *Birth of a Nation*, at fifty-nine in *Night of the Hunter*, at ninety in *The Whales of August*, and now that she is dead each seems as real as the other. It is we who grow old while they stay the same. Our feelings about everything may have changed completely from what they were in the 1950s. Sex, the sunlight and Saint-Tropez have decayed in their different ways and Bardot has become an old woman. But Juliette, the heroine of *And God Created Woman*, has been proved right, preserved on celluloid in all her youth, defying propriety and time with nothing but her pout and her insolent beauty.

Defiantly young: Brigitte Bardot in AND GOD CREATED WOMAN

Filmography

Le Trou normand (*Crazy for Love; Ti Ta To*), 1952; written by Arlette de Pitray; directed by Jean Boyer.

Manina, la fille sans voile (*The Girl in the Bikini; The Lighthouse Keeper's Daughter*), 1952; written by Xavier Vallier; directed by Willy Rozier.

Les Dents longues, 1952; written by Michel Audiard, Marcel Camus, Daniel Gélin and Jacques Robert; directed by Daniel Gélin.

Le Portrait de son père, 1953; written by André Berthomieu and Roger Pierre; directed by André Berthomieu.

Act of Love, 1953; written by Irwin Shaw and Joseph Kessel; directed by Anatole Litvak.

Si Versailles m'était conté (*Versailles*), 1953-4; written and directed by Sacha Guitry.

Tradita (*Night of Love*), 1954; written by Jules Daccar; directed by Mario Bonnard.

Helen of Troy, 1954; written by John Twist, Hugh Gray and N. Richard Nash; directed by Robert Wise.

Le Fils de Caroline Chérie, 1954; written and directed by Jean Devaivre.

Futures vedettes (*Sweet Sixteen*), 1955; written by Roger Vadim and Marc Allegrét; directed by Marc Allegrét.

Doctor at Sea, 1955; written by Nicholas Phipps and Jack Davies; directed by Ralph Thomas.

Les Grandes manoeuvres (*Summer Manoeuvres*), 1955; written by René Clair, Jérôme Géronimi and Jean Marsan; directed by René Clair.

La Lumière d'en face (*The Light Across the Street*), 1955; written by Louis Chavance and René Masson; directed by Georges Lacombe.

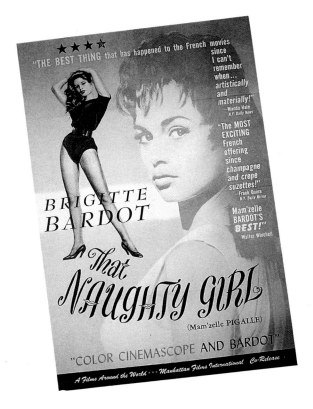

Cette sacrée gamine (*Mam'zelle Pigalle*), 1955; written by Roger Vadim and Michel Boisrond; directed by Michel Boisrond.

Mio figlio Nerone (*Nero's Weekend*), 1956; written by Rodolfo Sonego, Alessandro Continenza, Diego Fabbri and Ugo Guerra; directed by Stefano Vanzina.

En effeuillant la marguerite (*Plucking the Daisy; Please, Mr Balzac; Mam'zelle Striptease*), 1956; written by Roger Vadim and Marc Allegrét; directed by Marc Allegrét.

Et Dieu créa la femme (*And God Created Woman; And Woman … Was Created*), 1956; written by Roger Vadim and Raoul Lévy; directed by Roger Vadim.

La Mariée est trop belle (*The Bride is Much Too Beautiful; The Bride is Too Beautiful*), 1956; written by Philippe Agostini and Juliette Saint-Giniez; directed by Pierre Gaspard-Huit.

Une Parisienne (*Parisienne*), 1957; written by Annette Wademant and Jean Aurel; directed Michel Boisrond.

Les Bijoutiers du clair de lune (*The Night Heaven Fell; Heaven Fell that Night*), 1957; written by Roger Vadim and Peter Viertel; directed by Roger Vadim.

En cas de malheur (*Love is My Profession*), 1957; written by Jean Aurenche and Pierre Boast; directed by Claude Autant-Lara.

La Femme et le pantin (*The Female; A Woman Like Satan*), 1958; written by Jean Aurenche, Julien Duvivier, Marcel Achard and Albert Valentin; directed by Julien Duvivier.

Babette s'en va-t-en guerre (*Babette Goes to War*), 1959; written by Raoul Lévy and Gérard Oury; directed by Christian-Jaque.

Voulez-vous danser avec moi? (*Come Dance With Me*), 1959; written by Annette Wademant; directed by Michel Boisrond.

L'Affaire d'une nuit (*It Happened at Night*), 1960; written by Jean Aurenche and Henri Jeanson; directed by Henri Verneuil.

La Vérité *(The Truth)*, 1960; written by Henri-Georges Clouzot, and Jérôme Géronimi; directed by Henri-Georges Clouzot.

La Bride sur le cou *(Only for Love; Please Not Now!)*, 1961; written by Jean Aurel, Claude Brule and Roger Vadim; directed by Roger Vadim.

Les Amours célèbres, the **Agnès Bernauer** episode, 1961; written by France Roche; directed by Michel Boisrond.

Vie privée *(A Very Private Affair)*, 1961; written by Louis Malle and Jean-Paul Rappeneau; directed by Louis Malle.

Le Repos du guerrier *(Love on a Pillow; Warrior's Rest)*, 1962; written by Roger Vadim and Claude Choublier; directed by Roger Vadim.

Le Mépris *(Contempt)*, 1963; written and directed by Jean-Luc Godard.

Paparazzi, 1963; a documentary written and directed by Jacques Rozier.

Tentazioni proibite, 1963; a documentary directed by F. Oswaldo Civirani.

Une Ravissante idiote *(Adorable Idiot; Ravishing Idiot)*, 1963; written by Edouard Molinaro, Georges and André Tabet; directed by Edouard Molinaro.

Marie Soleil, 1964; written and directed by Antoine Bourseiller.

Dear Brigitte, 1965; written by Hal Kanter; directed by Henry Koster.

Filmography

Histoires extraordinaires, the **William Wilson** episode *(Spirits of the Dead; Tales of Mystery)*, 1967; written by Louis Malle and Daniel Boulanger; directed by Louis Malle.

Shalako, 1968; written by J. J. Griffith, Hal Hopper and Scot Finch; directed by Edward Dmytryk.

Les Femmes, 1969; written by Jean Aurel and Cécil Saint-Laurent; directed by Jean Aurel.

L'Ours et la poupée *(The Bear and the Doll)*, 1970; written by Nina Campaneez and Michel Deville; directed by Michel Deville.

Les Novices *(The Novices)*, 1970; written and directed by Guy Casaril.

Boulevard du rhum, 1970; written by Pierre Pelégri and Robert Enrico; directed by Robert Enrico.

Les Pétroleuses *(The Legend of Frenchie King)*; written by Clément Bowood, Guy Casaril and Daniel Boulanger; directed by Christian-Jaque, Guy Casaril.

Don Juan ou Et si Don Juan était une femme *(Don Juan or If Don Juan Were a Woman)*, 1973; written by Jean Cau, Roger Vadim and Jean-Pierre Petrolacci; directed by Roger Vadim.

L'Histoire très bonne et très joyeuse de Colinot Trousse-Chemise *(Colinot, the Skirt Puller-upper)*, 1973; written and directed by Nina Companeez.

Viva Maria!, 1965; written by Louis Malle and Jean-Claude Carrière; directed by Louis Malle.

Masculin-Féminin *(Masculine-Feminine)*, 1965; written and directed by Jean-Luc Godard.

A Coeur joie *(Two Weeks in September, 1967)*; written by Vahé Katcha, Pascal Jardin and Serge Bourguignon; directed by Serge Bourguignon.

Index

A

A Coeur joie 139, 186

Act of Love 184

Adair, Gilbert 16

Adjani, Isabelle 114

Adorable Idiot see Une Ravissante idiote

L'Affaire d'une nuit 185

Allégret, Marc 24, 26, 29, 38, 41, 44, 47, 49

Almendros, Nestor 41

Alpert, Hollis 54

Les Amours célébres (Agnès Bernauer episode) 185

And God Created Woman see Et Dieu créa la femme

Anouilh, Jean 33

Arendt, Hannah 15

Autant-Lara, Claude 68, 72, 78

B

Babette s'en va-t-en guerre (Babette Goes to War) 80, 185

Bardot, Anne-Marie ('Toti') 24, 29, 29, 30, 139

Bardot, Louis ('Pilou') 22, 29–30, 29, 139, 159

Bardot, Marie-Jeanne ('Mijanou') 22, 29, 30, 175

Barthes, Roland 8

The Bear and the Doll see L'Ours et la poupée

Beatty, Warren 148, 158

Beauvoir, Simone de 8, 18, 44, 48, 51, 68, 77, 80, 98, 108, 125–30, 158, 172, 176

Belmondo, Jean-Paul 114, 137

Bennett, Joan 72

Bergman, Ingrid 41

Berryman, John 98

Les Bijoutiers du clair de lune 64, 65–6, 67, 147, 171, 185

Birkin, Jane 143, *156–7*, 176

Bisset, Jacqueline 159

Bogarde, Dirk 35, 176

Bougrain-Dubourg (BB's lover) 175, 176

Boulevard du rhum 186

Bowie, David 178

Boyd, Stephen 65, 66, 67, 147

Boyer, Charles 65, 158

Brel, Jacques 114

The Bride is Much Too Beautiful see La Mariée est trop belle

The Bride is Too Beautiful see La Mariée est trop belle

La Bride sur le cou 185

Brien, Alan 10

Brigitte Bardot Foundation for the Protection of Animals 163, 181

Brozcek, Miroslav *174*, 175

Buñel, Luis 137

C

Camus, Albert 26, 47

Cardin, Pierre 133

Cardinale, Claudia 144

Carné, Marcel 41

Carter, Angela 68

Cette sacrée gamine 184

Chaplin, Charlie 16

Charrier, Jacques 80, 83, *84*, 93, *93*, 101, 139

Charrier, Nicolas 93, 160, 175, 178

Chevalier, Maurice 26

Christie, Julie 120

Clair, René 33, 41, 49

Clapton, Eric 178

Clouzot, Henri-Georges 94, 97, 98, 101, 108, 116, 147

Clown (spaniel) *161*

Cocteau, Jean 26

Colette 26

Colinot, the Skirt Puller-upper see L'Histoire très bonne et très joyeuse de Colinot Trousse-Chemise

Come Dance with me see Voulez-vous danser avec moi?

Connery, Sean 144, *146*, 147

Contempt *see Le Mépris*

Costello, Dolores 22

Coutard, Raoul 120

Coward, Noël 103

Crawford, Joan 22

Cukor, George 68, 108

Dali, Salvador 26

Dalle, Béatrice 26

Davis, Bette 18

Dean, James 69

Dear Brigitte 186

Delon, Alain 143

Dene, Terry 83

Deneuve, Catherine 47, 114, 120, 134, 137

Les Dents longues 184

Dépardieu, Gérard 114, 171

Dietrich, Marlene 8, 15–16, 22, 54, 152

Distel, Sacha *60, 61*, 80

Dmytryk, Edward 144

Doctor at Sea 34–5, 35, 184

Don Juan ou Et si Don Juan était une femme (Don Juan or If Don Juan Were a Woman) 152–8, *155, 156–7*, 186

d'Ormale, Bernard *see* Ormale, Bernard d'

Duras, Marguerite 10, 68, 93, 129–30, 148, 151, 176

Dylan, Bob 16

ℰ

Eastwood, Clint 144, 147

En cas de malheur 66, 69–75, *73, 74–5*, 78, 129, 140, 185

En effeuillant la marguerite 38, *39*, 184

Et Dieu créa la femme 9, 15, 16, 18, 33, 41–51, *45, 46, 48–9, 50, 52*, 54, *55*, 57, 66, 75, 78, 97, 101, 116, 123, 129, 140, 143, 158, 176, 184–5

Ewell, Tom 69

ℱ

Fellini, Federico 143

The Female see La Femme et le pantin

La Femme et le pantin 185

Les Femmes 186

Le Fils de Caroline Chérie 184

Fonda, Jane 47, 120, 125, 134, 148, 152, 158

Fossey, Dian 171

Frayn, Michael 8

Frey, Sami 94, *94–5*, 10

Futures vedettes 184

Gabin, Jean 66, 69, 72, *72–3*, 75, 78, *78–9*

Gable, Clark 69

Gainsbourg, Serge *142*, 143

Garbo, Greta 8, 10, 41, 116, 137, 152

Garland, Judy 108, 152

Genet, Jean 26

Gide, André 26, 47

Giraud, Odette 16

The Girl in the Bikini see Manina, la fille sans voil

Godard, Jean-Luc 44, 47, 90, 98, 120–5, *121*

Gouze-Rénal, Christine 175

Grable, Betty 2

Les Grandes Manoeuvres 32–3, 33, 51, 184

Grant, Cary 10

Greene, Graham 16

ℋ

Halsman, Philippe 172

Hawks, Howard 68

Hayworth, Rita 8, 15, 22, 57, 152

Heaven Fell that Night see Les Bijoutiers du clair de lune

Helen of Troy 41, 184

Henreid, Paul 18

Hepburn, Audrey 54, 137

Hepburn, Katharine 152

Heston, Charlton 65

L'Histoire très bonne et très joyeuse de Colinot Trousse-Chemise 158, 186

Histoires extraordinaires 'William Wilson' 143, *145*, 186

Horstig, Olga 17

Hughes, Howard 8

Hughes, Robert 77

Hupert, Isabelle 137
Huston, John 65, 68, 98
Hutton, Betty 152

It Happened at Night see L'Affaire
d'une nuit

Jagger, Mick 97
'Je dance donc je suis' 115
'Je me donne à qui me plaît' 115
'Je t'aime moi non plus' 143
Jules et Jim 51
Jurgens, Curt 41, 44, 49

K

Kael, Pauline 97, 98, 13
Kauffman, Stanley 125
Kerouac, Jack 69

Lake, Veronica 8, 152
Lamarr, Hedy 152
Lamont, Lena 108
Lang, Fritz 68, 72, 90, 120, 123,
    125
Lanzmann, Claude 129
Lazareff, Hélène 26
The Legend of Frenchie King see Les
    Pétroleuses
Lennon, John 175
Leone, Sergio 144

Levine, Joseph 120, 123
Lévy, Raoul 41, 61, 65, 66, 140
The Light Across the Street see La
    Lumière d'en face
The Lighthouse Keeper's Daughter see
    Manina, la fille sans voile
Logan, Joshua 68
Loren, Sophia 137
Losey, Joseph 137
Love is My Profession see En cas de
    malheur
Love on a Pillow see Le Repos du
    guerrier
Lowell, Robert 98
Loy, Myrna 18
La Lumière d'en face 184

M

Macdonald, Dwight 51
Mailer, Norman 68
Malle, Louis 103, 104, *107*, 108,
    116, 120, 130, 133, *134–5*,
    143, *145*, 176
Mamzelle Pigalle see Cette sacrée
    gamine
Mamzelle Striptease see En effeuillant
    la marguerite
Manckiewicz, Joseph 68
Manina, la fille sans voile 184
Manivet, Jean-Pierre 169
Mansfield, Jayne 15, 103
Marie Soleil 186
La Mariée est trop belle 185

Marquand, Christian 44, *55*
Martin, Dean 90
Masculin-Féminin 186
Mason, James 108
Mastroianni, Marcello 104, *104–5*,
    108
Matisse, Henri 77
Le Mépris 120–5, *121*, *122–3*, *124*,
    185
Miller, Arthur 98
Mio figlio Nerone 184
Monroe, Marilyn 9, 15, 54, 57,
    68–9, 98, 103, 137
Moravia, Alberto 120
Moreau, Jeanne 51, *91*, 114,
    130–4, 140, *141*, 143, 176
Morgan, Michèle 33

N

Nero's Weekend see Mio figlio Nerone
The Night Heaven Fell see Les Bijoutiers
    du clair de lune
Night of Love see Tradita
Les Novices (The Novices) 186
'Nue au soleil' 115

O

Olivier, Laurence 68
Onassis, Jacqueline 172
Only for Love see La Bride sur le cou
Ormale, Bernard d' 178, *180–1*,
    181–2
L'Ours et la poupée 186

P

Palance, Jack 120

Paparazzi 185

Une Parisienne (Parisienne) 10, 65,
    88, 125, 158, 160, 185

Perec, Georges 16

Les Pétroleuses 144, 186

Philipe, Gérard 33

Phillips, John 158

Piaf, Edith 26

Picasso, Pablo 76–7

Piccoli, Michel 90, 120, 123

Plath, Sylvia 98

Please Not Now! see *La Bride sur le cou*

Plemiannikov, Roger Vladimir *see*
    Vadim, Roger

Plucking the Daisy, Please; Mr Balzac
    see *En effeuillant la marguerite*

Poe, Edgar Allan 143

Polanski, Roman 137

Le Portrait de son père 184

Powell, William 18

Preminger, Otto 68

Presley, Elvis 83

Prévert, Jacques 26

R

Rappeneau, Jean-Paul 104

Une Ravissante idiote (Ravishing Idiot)
    185

Le Repos du guerrier 103, 185

Richard, Keith 97

Roberts, Glenys 148

Robles, Julio 171

Rojo (actor) 80

Russell, Jane 8

S

Sachs, Gunther *136*, 137–9, *137*,
    143, 147–8, 168, 175, 176

Sagan, Françoise 47, 152, 175, *177*

Sarles, Professor Henri 168

Sarne, Mike 139

Sartre, Jean-Paul 26, 47, 98

Seurat, Georges 77

Sexton, Anne 98

Shalako 143–8, *146*, 186

Si Versaille m'était conté 184

Signac, Paul 77

Simenon, Georges 69

Simon, Simone 24

Sinatra, Frank 61–5

Spada, Alain 18

Spirits of the Dead see *Histoires*
    extraordinaires 'William Wilson'

Stanwyck, Barbara 72

Steinem, Gloria 68

Sten, Anna 41

Sternberg, Josef von 8

Stewart, James 137

Stroyberg, Annette 83

Summer Manoeuvres see *Les Grandes*
    Manoeuvres

Sweet Sixteen see *Futures vedettes*

T

Tales of Mystery see *Histoires*
    extraordinaires 'William Wilson'

Tavernier, Bertrand 176

Temple, Shirley 16, 22, 175

Tentazioni proibite 185

Thomas, Ralph 35

Thompson, David 134

Townshend, Pete 175

Tradita 184

Trintignant, Jean-Louis 41, 44, *46*,
    47–8, *48–9*, *52*, 57, 61, 80, 83

Le Trou normand 6, 30, *31*, 49, 184

Truffaut, François 38, 44, 51, 108,
    137

The Truth see *La Vérité*

'Tu veux ou tu veux pas' 115

Turner, Lana 26

Two Weeks in September see *A Coeur*
    joie

Tynan, Kenneth 10

U

Updike, John 148

V

Vadim, Roger 6–8, 24, 26–30, *29*,
    38–41, *40*, 44–9, *46*, 53, 54,
    57, 61, 64, 65, 66, *67*, 72, 75,
    78, 80, 83, 101, *102–3*, 103,
    115, 120, 123, 125, 137, 139,
    143, 148, 152–8, 160, 175, 176

Verges, Laurent *153*

La Vérité 94–101, *94–5*, 116, 129, 140, 185

Versailles see Si Versaille m'était conté

A Very Private Affair see Vie privée

Vie privée 103–8, *104–5*, 116, 120, 185

Viertel, Peter 65

Viva Maria! 91, 130–4, *131, 132, 134–5*, 140, *141*, 144, 147, 159, 186

Voulez-vous danser avec moi? 185

W

Warrior's Rest see Le Repos du guerrier

Welch, Raquel 10

Welles, Orson 143

West, Mae 8

Wilder, Billy 68, 72

A Woman Like Satan see La Femme et le pantin

Wood, Natalie 69

Y

Young, Neil 175

Z

Zaguri, Bob 125, *126*

Zeldin, Theodore 148, 151

Picture   Acknowledgements

BFI Stills Posters and Design, London, with acknowledgement to Ascot Cineraid, Rome; Avco Embassy Pictures; CCM, Rome; CEIAP, Rome; Columbia Pictures; Compania Cinematografica Champion, Rome; Embassy Pictures Corp; Films de France; Filmsonor, Paris; Group Film Production; Iéna, Paris; Iéna/UCIL, Paris; Iéna/UCIL/Cocinor; Incom, Rome; Kingsley International; Les Films Concordia/Rome/Paris; Joseph E. Levine; Raoul J. Levy Productions; Lira Films, Paris; MGM; Miracle Films; Nouvelle Éditions de Films/Production Artistes Associés, Paris; Progefi-Cipra, Paris; J. Arthur Rank; Rizzoli Film, Rome; United Artists; Vides, Rome. Camera Press, London, with acknowledgement to Giancarlo Botti; Bert Cann; Loomis Dean; Jacques Harvey; Sam Levin; Patrick Morin; Piquemal; Monique Valentin. Gérard Cossevin. *Esquire*, March 1991/National Magazine Company Limited, London. Frank Spooner Pictures/Gamma with acknowledgement to Jean-Pierre Bonnotte; Eric Verdier; S. Veva Vigeveno. Frank Spooner Pictures/Stills. Ronald Grant Archive, London. Kobal Collection, London. Magnum Photos, London, with acknowledgement to Philippe Halsman, Nicholas Tikhomeroff. Photo Unifrance, Paris. Rex Features, London with acknowledgement to Giancarlo Botti; Tony Crawley; Emilio Lari; Tazio Secchiaroli; Goksin Sipahiogu; Sveeva Vigeveno. Rex Features/Sipa Press with acknowledgement to Aponte; Gilbert Ayoun; Alexandre/Pelletan/Boccon-Gibod; Michel Ginies; Patrick Morin; Yan Morvan; Edward Quinn; Tschaen. Sygma, London with acknowledgement to Giancarlo Botti; Jerome Briere; Dessalles; Philippe Ledru; Léonard de Raemy; G. Schachmes; Monique Valentin.